Milo Mahan

The Spiritual Point-of-View

Or, the glass reversed: an answer to Bishop Colenso

Milo Mahan

The Spiritual Point-of-View
Or, the glass reversed: an answer to Bishop Colenso

ISBN/EAN: 9783337425982

Printed in Europe, USA, Canada, Australia, Japan

Cover: Foto ©Lupo / pixelio.de

More available books at **www.hansebooks.com**

… The Spiritual Point-of-View; or,
The Glass Reversed.

AN ANSWER

TO

BISHOP COLENSO.

BY

M. MAHAN, D.D.

"Spiritual things are spiritually discerned."

NEW YORK:
D. APPLETON AND COMPANY,
443 & 445 BROADWAY
LONDON: 16 LITTLE BRITAIN.
1863.

ENTERED, according to Act of Congress, in the year 1863, by
D. APPLETON & CO.,
In the Clerk's Office of the District Court of the United States for the Southern District of New York.

PREFACE.

A WORD as to the circumstances under which this Tract was written may explain its general scope and object. I read Bishop Colenso's book. In conversation with a friend, I expressed my opinion of it, and showed where I thought its principal fallacy lay. The difficulty, I thought, was not so much in the arguments advanced by the writer, as in his habit of mind, his point-of-view, his *spirit*, in short, which is intensely infidel and materialistic. The answer to it should be in a different spirit. It should set forth, as clearly as possible, the opposite point-of-view. My friend was kind enough to say, that if I would write down briefly what I had said to him, without encumbering it with needless learning, it would probably be useful to many minds; and might do better service, in fact, than a more elaborate answer.

I have endeavored to act on the advice, simply writing down, without reference to any other book than the Bible, such thoughts as naturally arose in connection with the general subject. So far as Bishop

Colenso's fallacies arise from ignorance, I have touched them lightly : more learned Replies, from other pens, will do him ample justice in that respect. I have kept myself, in the main, to an exposure of that deeper and more subtle fallacy which underlies, not Bishop Colenso's argument merely, but all the objections advanced by the so-called science of the day.

M. MAHAN.

GENERAL THEOLOGICAL SEMINARY,
   December 19, 1862.

CONTENTS.

	PAGE
I.—BISHOP COLENSO'S POSITION,	7
II.—A FEW WORDS ON INSPIRATION,	12
III.—THE SIX DAYS OF CREATION; OR, THE TELESCOPE REVERSED,	22
IV.—INFALLIBILITY, COMMON SENSE, MATTER-OF-FACT,	34
V.—MOSES AND JOSHUA ADDRESSING ALL ISRAEL—EIGHT CHAPTERS OF DIFFICULTIES,	40
VI.—AN APOLOGY TO GOOD CHRISTIANS FOR THINGS NEW AND OLD,	52
VII.—JACOB'S FAMILY LIST,	57
VIII.—A FEW OTHER DIFFICULTIES,	62
IX.—SCRIPTURAL ARITHMETIC,	70
X.—FACTS BEARING UPON THE NUMBER OF THE ISRAELITES,	83
XI.—INFERENCE WITH REGARD TO THE HISTORICAL CHARACTER OF THE PENTATEUCH,	88
XII.—CONCLUDING REMARKS,	96
APPENDIX A.—THE FIRST-BORN COMPARED WITH THE WHOLE NUMBER OF ISRAELITES,	101
APPENDIX B.—THE NUMBERS OF HERODOTUS,	105

I.

BISHOP COLENSO'S POSITION.

Bishop Colenso's argument against the historical credibility of the Books of Moses is likely to make some noise in the world: not that it contains anything new, for his criticisms differ little in form or substance from those of innumerable infidels before him; but because it comes from a Bishop of the Church; and still more, because the writer professes to hold the Faith of Christ, while laboring to break down all belief in the sacred records which bear witness to that Faith.

He declares, indeed, that he does not stumble at "the miracles or supernatural revelations of Almighty God;" he "*could* believe and receive the miracles of Scripture heartily, *if only they were authenticated by a veracious history.*" Unfortunately, however, he does not find them to be so authenticated. The inference would seem to be, that he does not believe in "the miracles and supernatural revelations," and consequently, that he rejects the great mystery of the Incarnation and Resurrection. Yet, strange to say, the Bishop will not acknowledge any lack of faith in the essential Truth of Christianity. On the contrary, he seems to write and argue as if he still received it, as if he were firm in the true Faith of Christ, as if, in pursuing a line of argument by which, in his own words, "not the Pentateuch only, but the whole Bible," *may* be "removed," he were only "discharging a present duty to God and to the Church."

Now, we cannot enter the lists with such a writer, without a word of protest against the scandalous unfairness and inconsistency of the position he assumes.

It is the position of a sentinel who quietly opens one gate, or abandons one portion of the wall, to the enemy, protesting all the time that he is a true and zealous defender of the fortress; and that, though he may find it convenient to open all the gates and abandon the whole wall, it would yet be very harsh to suspect his fidelity as a watchman, or ask him to resign his post.

For the Bishop very plainly intimates that his criticisms are not to stop with the five Books of Moses. He says, *Preface*, p. 29:

"Should God, in His Providence, call me to the work, I shall not shrink from the duty of examining, on behalf of others, into the question, *in what way the Interpretation of the New Testament is affected* by the unhistorical character of the Pentateuch."

And if, on such examination, the New Testament also should be shown to be "unhistorical," what is to be done then? The Bishop answers:

"It is written on our hearts by God's own Finger, *as surely as by the hand of the Apostle in the Bible,* that God is, and is a rewarder of them that diligently seek him. * * * · The Light of God's Love did not shine less truly on pious minds when Enoch walked with God of old, *though there was then no Bible in existence,* than it does now."

It would appear, then, that no great harm will be done, and no great loss felt, if the Bible should be found wanting and be "removed" altogether. Nay, if we are to credit Bishop Colenso, some good may be expected from such a result: for, he says, there are certain passages in the Bible, bearing upon slavery and the treatment of slaves, which, to "a very intelligent Christian native" of South Africa, are positively revolting: see *Introductory Remarks,* p. 50. The Bible, therefore, had better be put out of court at once. But will the "very intelligent native" be satisfied with that? When you have removed his "difficulties" with regard to certain passages of the Scriptures, by proving the Scriptures generally to be unhistorical and unreliable, will he be more disposed to abide by that essential Truth which is proven from the Scriptures? The Bishop evidently thinks, not. He sees another step, necessary to be taken, and kindly hints to us what that step shall be—p. 36:

"I trust we shall not rest until *the system of our Church be reformed, and her boundaries at the same time enlarged;* to make her what a national Church should be, the Mother of spiritual life to *all* within the realm, embracing, as far as possible, all the *piety,* and *learning,* and *earnestness,* and *goodness* of the nation."

With the Bible "removed" from popular regard, and with the Church so "enlarged" as to admit everything in the nation except positive *belief*—for the Bishop is careful not to include *faith* among the things to be embraced—we shall have a system which even the "very intelligent native" of South Africa can approve.

Indulging such a hope, it would be but natural for the Bishop to join the ranks of those pious, learned, earnest, and good men, patrons of the Westminster Review and of the Infidel Press generally, by whom the same hope has been so long and so courageously maintained. But no: the Bishop of Natal sees no necessity for this.

"As a Bishop of the Church I *dissent entirely* from the principle laid down *by some*, * * * that we are bound by solemn obligations to maintain certain views * * * or, at least, to *resign our sacred office* in the Church, as soon as ever we feel it impossible to hold them."

He certainly puts it mildly, when he speaks of the "principle" as "laid down by *some*."

It is much as if he had said, "I dissent from the principle laid down by *some*, that when an officer holds a commission in the army, he is bound to maintain the cause to which he is sworn, or, at least, to resign." Now, we know that there are "some" who lay down this principle. Are there any who would venture openly to contravene it? Yes: the Bishop of Natal entirely dissents from it. Yet the Bishop, it would seem, is an honorable man. So sensitively moral is he, that the Bible shocks him continually; his conscience revolts from many of its precepts; his soul burns within him at the laxity and low views of those who labor to defend it; his Preface and Introduction fairly bristle with professions of "honesty" on his part, and with insinuations of dishonesty against the mass of his brethren of the Clergy. For, like the majority of his school, he regards no man as sincere who *takes pains* to solve the knotty questions of the Bible; or who, in cases which prove too hard for him, is willing to fall back upon simple faith. The only honest men, in the Bishop's estimation, are those who regard all explanations as mere evasions, unless they are satisfactory to everybody, and meet all possible objections. An ingenious solution is, to his mind, necessarily a false one. A learned solution is too elaborate and far-fetched. A solution which makes allowance for habits of mind and speech so peculiar and so remote from ours as were those of the sacred writers is set down at once as sophistical and evasive.

Now, in dealing with a critic who professes so high a standard of honesty and plain dealing, it is but fair to ask, What is his position in reference to the *great* questions which are involved in the discussion? And when we find that his position is in the highest degree equivocal—that he holds his place as a Bishop in conscious violation of his ordination vows—that he reconciles this sacrilege to his conscience by most palpable evasion of the meaning of plain words; when we find, in short, that he " dissents from " that common rule of honesty which compels a man in office either to acknowledge the obligations of that office, or else, at least, to resign, we surely cannot allow much weight to his professions of sincerity and plain dealing. Paine, in his " Age of Reason," makes similar professions of honesty and piety, on his part; he makes similar appeals to the piety and honesty of the reader.

II.

A FEW WORDS ON INSPIRATION.

I HAVE said, the Bishop and the Infidel are alike in their professions of piety and sincerity. If we examine a little farther, we shall find that there is no real difference in their arguments, or their object.

The object of both is to convict the Bible of so many mistakes in matters of fact, and of so many lapses, even in morality, that it shall lose all credit as *a Divine authority* in questions of religion.

In other words, they aim to demonstrate that the Scriptures are not *inspired*, in any such sense as would entitle them to be called *infallible*.

To prove this proposition, the method of both writers is substantially the same: the same fallacy underlies the arguments of both.

They take the words *infallible and inspired* in an absolute sense: not in any sense claimed by the Scriptures themselves, or admitted by the advocates of their infallibility.

Thus, to give a single instance from Bishop Colenso: speaking of the law regulating slavery, in Exod. xxi. 4, 20, 21, the writer observes, p. 50:

"I shall never forget the revulsion of feeling with which a very intelligent Christian native, with whose help I was translating these words into the Zulu tongue, first heard them as *words said to be uttered* by the same great and gracious Being, whom I was teaching him to trust in and adore. His whole soul revolted, &c. . . . I relieved his difficulty and my own for the present by telling him that . . . such words as these were written down by Moses, and *believed by him to have been divinely given to him*, because the thought of them arose in his heart, *as he conceived*, by the inspiration of God," &c.

Here the Bishop teaches his " Christian native " to reject the idea of a Divine Inspiration, when a single word from the Bible, explaining in what sense and for what purpose God gave the Law, would have removed the " difficulty," and would at the same time have protected the doctrine of Inspiration. For the Scriptures declare expressly that the Mosaic code was not given as a perfect law; that it was not meant to be a finality; that it was a mere provisional dispensation for a nation of stiff necks and hard hearts, who, if a better law had been given, would have absolutely refused it. Apply this truth to the enactment in Exod. xxi. 21. It was undoubtedly hard on slaves, that a master might chastise them with any degree of severity, *provided only* that he should not cause them *to die under his hand*. But was not this proviso an improvement on the law, or custom, that existed before? Was it not a merciful addition to the practice that prevailed generally among the most enlightened nations of antiquity? Among the Romans, a master, if he chose, might kill his slave outright. Indeed, a father had similar power of life and death over his son. If Moses, therefore, reduced this power a little in the case of the Jews, and made their law of slavery more humane than that of other nations; if, in short, he made the law as good as they could bear, was there anything in all this to preclude the idea of Inspiration?

But the Bishop objects to those severities in the law which Moses still left in it. Had it been given by God, he thinks, it would have been freed altogether from *every* objectionable feature. A slave would not have been spoken of as *mere* " money." A master would not have been allowed " to go unpunished, because the victim of the brutal usage survived a few hours."

Now, there is a vast difference between saying that a slave *is his* master's *money*, and saying that he is "*mere* money;" as much so as there is between calling a working man an *operative* and calling him a *mere* operative. The latter phrase, in both instances, is one of disparagement. The former only expresses in plain words a serviceable relation. But, to let this pass, does Bishop Colenso think that God never speaks, without speaking *His whole mind?* If so, his notion of Inspiration is directly the reverse of that which is laid down in the Scriptures. Nothing is more certain than that the Bible professes to be a *gradual* revelation : that *line upon line, and precept upon precept, here a little and there a little,* each later portion being an advance upon the parts preceding, is the plan upon which its vast system of instruction is built up. And common sense assures us that this plan is the only rational one, in dealing with frail men, and the only one that can be called in any true sense Divine. Draco gave the Athenians a code of laws so just that no man could endure them. Solon gave them a code which they were able to bear. Which was the more God-like of the two legislators? Which had the larger share of that gracious light, that light of celestial wisdom illumining but not confounding, which shines from the Face of the merciful Father of Mankind?

But to return to the main point: What has been shown in this example is true of Bishop Colenso's reasoning in general. He is possessed with the idea that Inspiration, as predicated of the Scriptures, can never inspire the utterance of half-truths, or truths imperfectly expressed, or truths needing the light of other truths to make them intelligible. In short, because God is perfect, everything that comes from him must needs be perfect also. Though all nature is a riddle, and yet comes from God; though the human mind is a riddle, and yet reflects His image; though man, in his highest illumination, can see but darkly, as through a darkened glass: yet the Divine word—*because* it comes from God,—must have no riddles in it, no seeming contradictions, no difficulties, no opaque spots, no paradoxes, nothing that the unlearned and unstable can wrest to their own destruction.

The Scriptures lay claim to no such Inspiration. Nor does any advocate of the Scriptures contend for anything of the kind. We claim that *all* Scripture is given by Inspiration of God; that the sacred writers spake, "not by the will of man," but "as they were moved by the Holy Ghost;" that there is nothing in the Bible which is not "profitable," if rightly understood; and consequently, that, though some portions of the Word may be more edifying than others, yet every portion has the Divine sanction, and, whether true or not from *all* points of view, whether true or not considered in itself, is infallibly true from the spiritual point of view; that is, considered in its bearing upon the aim and purport of the Scriptures in general.

But does this claim imply that there are to be no difficulties in Scripture? Not at all. Difficulties are inherent in all literature: and the Bible, being not a Book merely, but a vast literature, and a literature belonging to an age, and people, and tongue, of which we know little from other sources, must, in the nature of things, present peculiar and almost insuperable difficulties. It is enough that these difficulties occur chiefly in questions of literary or scientific curiosity, which may be decided this way or that, without in the least affecting the main object for which the Scriptures were written.

For example, there are corruptions and interpolations in Scripture, some known to be such, and some (perhaps) unknown. There are also Books, such as Job, which may be matter-of-fact history, or *may* be poetry of that kind which is *the spirit* of history. There are also certain narratives, evidently historical, —the Creation, for example, or the Deluge,—which are yet so couched in idiomatic or symbolic phrases that wise interpreters have doubted, from Origen's day downward, whether they mean what on the surface they seem to mean. On this point, I shall have more to say presently. It will be enough to say here that, should a sound criticism eventually add to the number of known interpolations; should the Books now thought to be sacred dramas be proved to be such; should it be demonstrated, by learned examination, that the more ancient parts of the Bible need to be translated, not merely from the Hebrew into English, but from Hebrew popular idioms into the idioms of an age more arithmetical and exact—still, nothing is proved against either the Truth or the Divine Inspiration of the Scriptures. We merely learn to drop those portions which are interpolated, and to leave them out of the account. And as to other portions, we may have to abandon a surface sense, which is of no particular importance, and to take in its stead a deeper and more spiritual sense.

But, it may be asked, would it not have been better to have *so* inspired the Scriptures as to leave no place for difficulties of the kinds above-mentioned?

I answer, No. Of the two principal courses which Inspiration might take with a view to benefit all ages, the course that has actually been taken is decidedly the better.

Inspiration *might* have enabled one, two, or three minds to write in one great book, and in language scientifically correct, a revelation of Divine Truth in which no contradiction, or seeming contradiction, could possibly have been detected. In such a case, as it would be necessary, not only to make the book perfect, but to keep it so, a perpetual miracle would have been needed to guard against those verbal errors, omissions, corruptions, and interpolations to which all writings are subject in the lapse of time. Another perpetual miracle would have been needed to enable translators to do their work aright. A third perpetual miracle would have been needed in behalf of interpreters. For it is obvious that a work *scientifically* accurate may be spoiled by the least error, or blemish, or misinterpretation. The introduction of a single *iota* into the Nicene Creed, for example, would change the Truth of God into an Arian lie. And if a great Book were written with the scientific precision of the Nicene Creed, nothing short of a standing miracle could keep it free from corruptions of the most unmanageable kind.

Besides which, such a Book, if written, would never have been read. To the mass of men, it would have been less intelligible, and less interesting, than Aristotle's Ethics.

Rejecting this course, therefore, as unadapted to the great end in view, Inspiration took another and a wiser course. It inspired many minds, in many ages, to write many books, in many varieties of style, the work growing to such a bulk that the errors of copyists, translators, and interpreters, with all the blots and blemishes of time, are practically neutralized in the greatness of the whole. Thus, all the sewers of earth empty into the ocean, yet the ocean is not defiled. All of earth's vapors steam up into the sunshine, yet the sunshine remains pure. On the same principle, the very bulk of the Sacred Writings, their variety, their exuberance of life, their luxury of detail, their half-truths in one place dovetailing so admirably into half-truths in another, their broken lines here so marvellously pieced out by broken lines there, in short, the wondrous harmonies that come out from so many seeming discords—this vastness and manifoldness of the inspired Literature secures it, *without miracle*, against suffering, as a whole, from its occasional corruptions. It is so inspired as to be self-adjusting, self-purifying, and, to those who consult it on its own principles, self-interpreting. It has salt enough in it to sweeten, not merely its own waters, but any foreign admixture that may accidentally flow in.

A man of moderate wealth is obliged to have his property insured. A millionnaire has so much, and such varied property, that it insures itself. There is something of the same principle in the riches of the Divine Oracles. Their superabundant variety—to say nothing of other features—constitutes, as it were, a policy of self-insurance.

To speak without metaphor, it is worthy of God, and in consonance with all we know of the character of God, that, if He condescends to inspire men at all, He should inspire them *as men speaking to men:* not as critics, not as word-catchers, not as grammarians, not as arithmeticians, not as logicians; but simply as true men, speaking truths, which, for the most part, were in advance of their age, but which had to be couched in the mind and idiom of the age to which they spoke. Men thus inspired would of course speak imperfectly, and in a certain sense, inaccurately. This being granted, it is again worthy of God, that He—knowing the imperfections and inaccuracies of human mind and human speech—should find the remedy in a vast variety of utterances, complementing, explaining, and guarding one another, rather than in one scientifically exact utterance, which nought but a perpetual miracle could keep exact.

Besides which, an inspired book for men ought to be a readable book—a pleasant book to read. The Bible is such. It has been more read, oftener quoted, better remembered, than all other books put together. But if it had been written to suit critics and word-catchers, nobody else would have touched it.

Besides which, again: an inspired book ought to be a book to make men think. But no book really serves this purpose unless it deals in hints, and half-utterances, and seeming paradoxes, as well as in open manifestations of the truth. A perfectly easy book to read is read once and no more. It is read, not studied. The Bible is so written as to stimulate study: more so than any other book or books known to mankind.

Besides which, once more: a book coming from God ought to be in a certain analogy with Nature, which is also His book. But Nature, we know, abounds in difficulties, paradoxes, and seeming contradictions. Bishop Butler has demonstrated that the difficulties of the Bible and those of Nature are in a wonderful way analogous, and complementary to one another.

For these and like reasons, the plan of inspiring a great literature, and of inspiring it in such a way as to make it a catholic literature, capable of translation into all languages without risk of serious error, seems better and wiser than any other imaginable plan.

But a plan like this necessarily involves a theory of Inspiration in accordance with it.

It involves not perfection in any one part, considered in itself; as, for example, that the historical books should be "historical," in *the modern sense* of the word. A perfectly true history may contain admixtures which require a sound and cautious criticism to determine whether they are literal facts or symbolic representations of large groups of facts. And we know that early historians delighted in such admixtures. On the other hand, a history may be quite accurate in dates and matters of fact, yet, taken as a whole, may convey an enormous lie. We are accustomed in modern times to this latter style of history. *Our* canon of the "historical" excludes everything but literal facts. But mankind, in primitive times, acknowledged no such canon. Where we philosophize in reflections, they philosophized in symbols. This, of course, creates a difficulty in dealing with early writers. It renders it necessary for the interpreter to be constantly on his guard. We have to enter, not merely into words, but if possible into mind, quite different in all its habits from the mere modern mind. Our great effort, in short, is, in dealing with ancient writings, to put ourselves to the utmost at the ancient point-of-view. And if those writings should be sacred, as well as ancient, the difficulty in some points may, for a long time at least, be absolutely insuperable.

Now, Bishop Colenso, like other skeptics, allows for nothing of this sort. He assumes a modern, rationalistic, matter-of-fact point-of-view. From that he frames his own theory of Inspiration. From that he lays down his own canons of the "historical." What accords not with these canons he calls "unhistorical." What he calls "unhistorical," he therefore judges to be "uninspired."

The assumption underlies the whole of his argument. I shall be obliged to recur to it more than once, to make my meaning clear. For the present, I will endeavor to illustrate it by considering one of the first and chief "difficulties" in the Historical Books of Moses.

III.

THE SIX DAYS OF CREATION; OR, THE TELESCOPE REVERSED.

The Mosaic account of the creation of the world is not in harmony with the results of scientific investigation.

It is, therefore, not a true account.

It is, therefore, not entitled to be called an *inspired* or *infallible* account.

Such is the position of the Infidel,* contemplating the Scriptures from what he calls a scientific point-of-view. In answering the objection, I will not question the results of modern investigation. I will assume on trust—for, not being a student of science, I *know* nothing about it—that the world was originally a chaos, a huge bulk of seething mist; that in the course of millions of ages it cooled down to something approaching to its present size and form; that in millions of ages more, light penetrated the opaque atmosphere, and vast wedges of flinty rock emerged from the heaving

* Bishop Colenso merely alludes to this and other difficulties connected with Science. I have given a larger space to it, because it enables me to illustrate, more fully than other instances, the difference between a spiritual and a material point-of-view.

waters; that in other millions of ages the rock clothed itself in soil, and the soil adorned itself with a rich plumage of vegetable life; that in millions of ages more, other rocks formed, and other soils appeared, with other and varied garbs, while the waters teemed with the lower forms of animal life, and from the waters the skies were colonized, and strange amphibious creatures crawled out upon the land; that finally, millions of ages still revolving, with new layers of rock and soil, the higher orders of animal life appeared, and among them rose up one who was destined to be their king, a creature not pachydermatous or strong-clawed, but thin-skinned and defenceless, and, except for a big brain and flexile tongue, the most helpless thing that moved.

All this, I say, I will *suppose* to be in substance true. But if true, God, when He inspired Moses, knew it to be true. Why, then, did He inspire his servant to write for all ages an account which in matter-of-fact points seems to differ from all this?

I answer that, if the above account be true, God knew it to be true. But He knew also that, in course of time, man would find it out for himself. There was no need then of a matter-of-fact *revelation*. Moreover, if such a revelation should be made to the age of Moses, the age would reject it, not being prepared for it; and the whole scheme of Inspiration would be strangled at the birth. But, while a matter-of-fact revelation would be needless, some revealed account might be useful, to guard the people of God against the false and foolish cosmogonies of the heathen.

Here, then, is reason enough at once, not for inspiring a false account of Creation, but for clothing the true account in language and ideas suited to the age.

If I wished to give a young child a *true* notion of the distance of the sun, I would not tell him the sun is millions of miles away; it would answer the purpose better to say *hundreds* of miles. For a child has some idea of what hundreds mean. The word millions would only serve to bewilder and perplex him.

But further: if God knew the above account of Creation to be the true one; and if He knew, moreover, that man would find it out; He also knew that the discovery, when made, would be perilous to man's faith. The idea of millions on millions of ages is so vast, so far beyond all finite imagination, that it seems almost to run into the idea of *Eternity* itself. Indeed, human language can describe Eternity only by accumulations of terms, which really are descriptive of Time, and Time only. We say Sæcula Sæculorum— ages of ages—the very term that describes the geological eras. There is a danger, then, that when the finite mind begins to contemplate Time as *practically* an infinite duration, it should slide into the easy error of regarding it as really infinite. A world so old as ours seems, to all intents and purposes, a world without beginning. It seems virtually eternal. The notion of a Maker, if not absolutely banished, is at all events put so far off, that it becomes vague and inoperative. In short, the Creature, by being clothed in these stupendous figures, assumes a bulk and mysterious grandeur which effectually shuts out the view of the Creator.

Again: the notion of slow and long-continued growth, of that growth by which continents are built up in millions of years from the bottoms of great seas, is one that appals and almost stupefies the mind. Of course, it is not really inconsistent with the idea of *One who speaks and it is done,* but practically it renders that idea extremely difficult to entertain. The more it takes hold of the mind, the more it inclines us to put Growth for God: to adopt some theory of development, and in the height of scientific exaltation to relapse into the philosophy of poor Topsey, and to say of the whole world, " It was not made but grew."

Again: the human point-of-view is always practically to the mind a *central* point-of-view. Whichever way we look, the horizon is equi-distant around us; and the ages past are necessarily the measure of the ages yet to come. Science reveals to us billions of years behind. How can we help expecting billions of years before us ? The great lesson of Science is that " all things continue now as they were from the beginning." The same minute shell-fish which built up so large a portion of the land that now is, are working in Ocean's depths as industriously as ever. Niagara, after sawing its way up through the rock some millions of years, has hardly yet accomplished more than half of its day's work. The great ice rivers of the North, which have supplied the world with boulders, are still crawling on at the same snail's pace. " Where, then, is the promise of His coming ? " What prospect is there, that a world which has lasted so long, and is still so vigorous, shall ever come to an end ?

Science, in this way, does not teach infidelity. I accuse it of nothing of the sort. The true man of science is also a man of faith : and as physical ideas loom up, in his telescope, in proportions of overwhelming bulk and grandeur, he has the wisdom to reverse the telescope, and to look at them occasionally from the spiritual point-of-view. The glass which magnifies a flea into an elephant, can likewise *minify* an elephant into a flea. Science, therefore, is not necessarily a fosterer of unbelief. Infidelity is the resort of mere sciolists, of men who look at things only from one point-of-view, of men who (as the Wise Man says, Eccles. iii. 11) have " the *world so set* in their heart" that they cannot " find out the work that *God* maketh."

Still, as the mass of men are impatient and one-sided, easily satisfied with one glance at a truth, science is unquestionably perilous to Faith. It exalts the creature, and so far tends to disparage the Creator. It fixes the eye upon the greatness of material things, and so far tends to blind us to spiritual things.

Now, to return to the argument: if God, in the days of Moses, foresaw the brilliant results of modern investigation; if He foresaw that man would make discoveries which, contemplated from a human point-of-view, would be perilous to his Faith, then it would not become God, as a Father, to ante-date these dangerous discoveries. Sufficient unto the day is the evil thereof. The trial of the nineteenth century would come soon enough. So far as He thought proper to teach man a cosmogony, He would teach it in such terms as would be the most edifying and least dangerous. He would teach it also in terms which, if not scientifically exact, should be found, when the time came, to be at least true in substance: true from the spiritual, if not from the material, point-of-view.

Hence the main features of the First Chapter of Genesis. There is a chaos; *then* breath, motion, light, vivifying the chaos; *then* waters separating from waters, clouds above and the great sea beneath; *then* the dry land emerging from the waters, and clothing itself in grass, and herb, and fruit tree yielding fruit; *then* light holders (according to the Hebrew) in the firmament of the heavens; *then* life in the waters, in the air, and in the earth ; *then* higher types of life, not water-bred and oval, but earth-bred and mammal, from amid which, by a special creation and special gift, cometh lordly man.

So far the account is true from every point-of-view. Science may enlarge it and enrich it, but to improve it is impossible.

Moreover, there is a beautiful gradation* in these successive acts. "It is evening and it is morning," as each follows each. There are no abrupt transitions. It is not *day* following *night*, and *night* following *day*, but it is Day rolling into Day, as the long waves of the sea roll into one another, following ever the line of beauty, running down the curved slope of Evening, and up the curved steep of Morning, a succession of teeming periods continuous but distinct.

If Science teaches anything, it teaches substantially the same lesson.

But then, to mark these periods, the word *Day* is used: and a Day, scientifically, is but twenty-four hours, a diurnal revolution of the earth upon its axis. I wonder it never occurs to these word-catchers, that as a pure matter of fact the earth *has no axis;* and that Science, at some future day, may catch *them* tripping in their speech even as they catch Moses. But,

* Hugh Miller, in his *Testimony of the Rocks*, seems to assume a succession of catastrophes. I believe, however, that the general drift of science favors the idea of a *continuous* series of ages running gradually into one another.

to let this pass : is it not a sufficient answer that the word *Day*, not only in Scripture but in all human writings, is perfectly *capable* of being used in an unscientific sense ? And if it is capable of being so used, we are not bound in any case to confine its meaning, unless the nature of that case should seem to require it.

Above all, is it not sufficient that an inspired writer of the New Testament, 2 Pet. iii. 3–8, foreseeing that there would " come in the last days scoffers," and that the burden of their scoffing would be the great maxim of modern science—" all things continue as they were from the beginning of creation,"—distinctly refers for their confutation to the great act of creation, and reminds them, *in that connection*, that " one day is *with the Lord* as a thousand years, and a thousand years as one day " ?

The Apostle refers them, in other words, to the contemplation of Time from a Divine point-of-view.

And so I come to the main question before us. It is simply this :

If God foreknew that man would at some day discover a cosmogony such as that which Geology professes to have found ; and if He foresaw that this cosmogony, from the vastness of its numbers and the bulk of its physical ideas, would prove perilous to Faith ; what, humanly speaking, would be the best mode of guarding against this danger ?

I answer : the best way would be—of course, I speak humanly—to furnish man beforehand with a cosmogony, which should enable him, as it were, to reverse the telescope, and to contemplate creation from the Divine point-of-view.

In our eyes, a billion of years is a very great matter. In God's eyes it is a very small matter. With us the duration of Time seems hardly short of an eternity. With God, it is a mere breath, a mere vapor, a passing thought, a thing of infinitely less duration than the word, " Let there be light." For heaven and earth pass away, but His word passeth not away. However long a time, therefore, the world was in making or in growing, yet let the scoffer remember that a word of God is something which endures still longer: for "*by the word* of God the heavens were of old, and the earth standing out of the water and in the water . . . . and, *by the same word*, the heavens and the earth . . . . are kept in store."

A cosmogony written from this point-of-view would necessarily be couched in phrases opposite, though not contradictory, to " the great swelling words " of Science. " Periods " would dwindle into " Days." The " Ages of Transition," which link the Periods, would appear but as " Evenings " or " Mornings." In short, the glass being reversed, the object contemplated through it would remain the same: only it would be presented in *miniature*.

Such a picture, moreover, would not merely *not contradict*, it would modify, correct, fill up, the cosmogonies of natural science.

And wonderfully is this end attained by the simple narrative of the Bible.

Science puts " the beginning " so far back, that human thought can hardly reach it. Revelation brings it right up before the eyes. Science goes out in quest of God; but the journey is so long, through ages upon ages, that the wings of thought flag, and she fails to come near Him. Revelation begins with God, and, in

Him and His strength, finds the ages to be nothing. Armed with the first verse of Genesis, we meet Science face to face, and announce to her what she seeks, but never of herself can find, that "in the beginning God created the heavens and the earth."

In the same way: when she begins to talk to us of the æons, or ages, tracing their weary length of arithmetical duration, we remind her (with St. Paul, Heb. xi. 3) that their vastness is no obstacle to Faith: for "by Faith we understand that the *Ages* (æons) were framed by *the Word of God;*" and in His word, and His Life, the longest periods are mere Days, such as Moses has described them.

So again: when she holds up an illimitable future, we tell her that this future has an appointed end. God worked six days, preparing the way for man. On the seventh day God rested and commanded man to work. "I have made the earth: do you replenish and subdue it. I have planted a garden: do you dress it and keep it." An eighth day is coming, in which, man's work being accomplished, he also shall rest.

Thus, Science is not destroyed: it is simply filled up. What it cannot reveal, Inspiration reveals for it: what it can reveal, Inspiration substantially confirms, translating it, however, from human language into Divine, and so enabling us to contemplate it, not from a human, but from a Divine, point-of-view.

Now, to go back from this digression to the subject of the chapter immediately preceding: The infidels *assume* that the cosmogony of Moses was meant to be a revelation. So far I agree with them. They assume further, that it was meant to be a revelation from the earthly, or matter-of-fact, point-of-view. There I differ with them. It is an assumption utterly at variance with the whole object of Inspiration.

I will merely add, that the Divine point-of-view is of such infinitely great importance, in comparison with the human, that if in the sacred Books the latter were neglected altogether, we should have no reason to complain. But it is a characteristic of God's works, that they are thrifty in the use of means, and are often made to combine objects the most diverse from one another. Thus, to take one example out of many, the human mouth is the organ of the divine faculty of speech, and is at the same time the instrument of the brute faculty of nutrition. The most spiritual act of man, and the most sensuous, are equally well performed by one and the same organ. The same tongue, teeth, lips, and palate, which seem to be made expressly for speech and song, are as exquisitely adapted to the uses of deglutition. On the same principle, I regard it as a mark of the Divine Hand in Sacred Scripture, that while in all cases the spiritual end comes first, and the spiritual point-of-view is the true stand-point of interpretation, yet incidentally all Scriptures admit of profitable interpretations from other points-of-view, and may be applied without violence in a variety of ways.

Thus the First Chapter of Genesis was not intended, in the first place, to teach a scientific cosmogony. But I find that, incidentally, it does give a wonderfully correct outline of that science, so far, at all events, as the science is reliable. The geologist traces the work of creation in substantially the same order, and same progression, as that which Moses gives. He differs only in the apparent length or number of the intervals assigned. But even in this matter, the geologist adds no definite information. Where Moses speaks of Days, he speaks of Periods. And if I ask what a Period is, I find that it is substantially what a Day is, in its larger Scriptural sense, namely any duration of time that has a beginning, a middle, and an end. In all essentials, then, Moses agrees with the Geologist.

But furthermore I find that, incidentally, the six Days of Moses have a wonderful correspondence with the six Days or Periods of sacred History that preceded the Christian era. There was the Adamic Day, terminating with the judgment upon the Serpent; the Noachic Day, with the judgment of the Flood; the Abrahamic Day, with the destruction of Sodom and Gomorrah; the Mosaic Day, with the ruin of the Egyptians; the Prophetic Day, with the Captivity in Babylon; the Evangelic Day, with the appearing of the Second Man, and the destruction of Jerusalem. Last of all comes the seventh Day, the Day of Christianity, in which God rests from His work "finished" on the Cross, and having secured man his inheritance, commands him to "dress and keep it."

Now a skeptic, I dare say, would laugh at such manifoldness of meaning attributed to one passage. He laughs because his stand-point is different from mine. But I submit that if I, from my stand-point, can see in this noble chapter, in the first place a high Theology, in the second a broad Philosophy, in the third a true Science, and in the fourth a key to History, while in all I discern the marks of a Divine Inspiration, I have decidedly the advantage of one who sees in it nothing more than a fine old legend of the hoar antiquity of the Jews.

At all events, I can safely say to the skeptic, your

"difficulties" are not in the doctrine of Inspiration: they are merely in the stand-point from which you look. Change your stand-point, and the difficulties will vanish.*

* Rorison, in his *Creative Week*, one of the Oxford *Replies to Essays and Reviews*, shows that the first chapter of Genesis is *poetical* in style and structure. For this he has been censured by some, as if the admission involved a doubt of the reality of the Mosaic narrative. But, as he well observes, " Poetry may be detached from reality, or opposed to reality: it may also, and that without ceasing to be itself, or foregoing its appropriate framework, be the *highest and most vivid exponent of reality.*" In the same spirit, the late Dr. Turner, one of the safest and least fanciful of interpreters, inclines to the opinion that the Temptation and Fall, Gen. iii., is clothed in language partly allegorical; and he proves that such an admission does not compromise in the least the historical truth of the narrative: *Companion to the Book of Genesis*, pp. 183–196. In such cases, it is the part of sound critics to determine *how far* the historian avails himself of poetical or allegorical expressions. That Eve, for example, was tempted and fell, and that there was a tempter outside of her own heart and mind, is clear on any honest rendering of Gen. iii. Whether the tempter was a literal serpent, or Satan speaking through a serpent, or Satan assuming the form of a serpent, or Satan acting in that insidious and subtle way of which the serpent is the symbol, has always been more or less of an open question. We unconsciously spiritualize the interpretation so far as to believe—though Moses says nothing to that effect—that Satan was in some way or other the real tempter.

IV.

INFALLIBILITY, COMMON SENSE, MATTER-OF-FACT.

I HAVE said so much on the fallacy connected with Inspiration, that I may dismiss the term *infallible* with a few brief remarks.

Bishop Colenso uses the word in an arbitrary sense: in a sense which can by no possibility apply to a great *literature*, such as that which is included in the Bible.

Literature is thought clothed in language; and language, in itself, is always fallible. The most precise phrases convey different shades of meaning to different minds. Words, like leaves on trees, not only rise and fall—as Horace beautifully says,—but are constantly undergoing an imperceptible change of tint. Phrases in one tongue can hardly ever find their equivalents in another. In the most polished and perfect speech there are idioms, intelligible enough to those who daily use them, but to a stranger who takes them literally, positively absurd. A Londoner will say that "*everybody* is gone out of town;" or a Parisian will remark that "*all the world*" is invited to somebody's reception," without thinking that a word-catcher of some future age may find, in those phrases, proof positive that Londoners and Parisians were little better than Cretans. Instances of the same kind will occur to every reader.

Now, if we consider that the Bible is popular in its style; that it comes to us from the most ancient of all tongues, and the most intensely idiomatic; that it is the growth of many ages, each with its own peculiarities of thought and of expression; that the language from which it sprang died in giving it birth; that, in short, it addresses us with a modern and English look, but with a soul profoundly ancient and Oriental, it must be plain that such a Book can be infallible solely on one positive and indispensable condition.

Its infallibility applies only to its meaning. But, happily, its meaning is made clear, in all essentials of revelation, not only by concurrent testimony in the living voice of the Church, but by that manifoldness of expression, that *line upon line*, and *precept upon precept*, of which I have already spoken in the chapter on Inspiration.

It is infallible *in the spirit*, not in the letter. But to get at the spirit of any book, we must interpret the parts of it by the whole, not the whole by parts arbitrarily taken.

Not to dwell on considerations of this kind, it will be enough to say, that the Bible comes to us accompanied by a body of living interpretation; that interpretation is necessarily a growing science, being the fruit of the loving labor, not of one mind or one age, but of all minds in the Church and all ages; that its rules, principles, and safeguards, being warranted by the common sense of Christendom, and laid down in plain terms by the sacred Book itself, constitute as it were the spiritual stand-point, from which alone things spiritual can be properly discerned.

Now Bishop Colenso chooses a stand-point of his

own. Brought up in a School of "private interpretation," with no faith in the Church, he is a victim of that popular *bibliolatry*, which consists in a worship of the letter of the Scriptures, without any corresponding reverence for the "authority" which (Art. xx.) is the divinely appointed "witness and keeper of Holy Writ."

Nor is he the less a bibliolatrist, in that he now chooses to abuse the idol to which he has hitherto fallen down. All idolaters do the same, at times. If their fetishes fail to help them, according to their own wishes, the next step often is to tear the fetish in pieces.

When the Bible is used as a private oracle, a sort of "ephod and teraphim" (Judges xvii. 5-13) for the worship of self-will, it is naturally expected to give such answers as the owner of it may desire. But the inspired word is too "lively" to bend long to such demands. The owner, perhaps, has some fanatical notion about Slavery: but the Bible, in spite of every pressure, fails to humor the notion. What is its votary to do? He concludes, with Bishop Colenso,* that on *that* particular point the Inspiration is wanting. Or his brain is vexed with an enthusiasm for the Total-abstinence cause. But the Bible, on this subject, is favorable to no extremes. On *that* point, then, Inspiration is "behind the age." Or, it may be, he has fallen into a scientific mania. The Bible, on the whole, does not flatter human science, seeming almost to consider it a species of child's play. On *that* point, then, Inspiration is manifestly at fault. Or he is enamored of "facts," and "dates," and arithmetical "calculations." Well:

Introduction, p. 50.

the Bible uses "facts" as but secondary to Truth; about "dates" it seems indifferent, and hardly conscious of their importance; and, as to arithmetic, its "rule of three" was certainly not learned in any of our common schools. All this is puzzling to a *mere* matter-of-fact mind. It is not precisely in harmony with the mind of our own age. It denotes a point-of-view to which we are little accustomed. The consequence is that if we *will* insist on having an answer in our own way, and on our own terms, the oracle that we consult disappoints us, and puts us out; and, like Naaman the Assyrian, we turn from it in a rage.

In such cases, feeling ourselves to be substantially* in the right, we wonder that the Bible does not go with us to all extremes. We forget that Inspiration may be given for the very purpose of moderating our extremes: teaching us, that "slavery," for example, may be a good thing in its "time;" that "total abstinence" may be an excellent discipline, but pernicious if made a duty of obligation; that "facts" and "figures," after all, are but the skeleton of Truth, needing flesh and blood and life to make them endurable.

And such, I think, is the essence of Bishop Colenso's error. Instead of consulting the Bible on its own terms, and according to its own law, he makes a private oracle of it, and so finds it fallible. He tries it, not by Catholic rules, but by principles and rules vehemently Colensic. He interprets it, not by the common sense of the Church, but by Bishop Colenso's sense—or by that of some "intelligent Christian native," a disciple of Bishop Colenso.

* I say "substantially;" for there is generally a right feeling even in the most fanatical notions.

The fallacy is too common with all classes of thinkers. The appeal to the "intelligent Christian native," like the appeal so often made to "some plain, unlettered farmer," is, in reality, an appeal to that impartial personage whom we more properly call "Self." The "farmer" will generally answer us very much as we wish to have him answer: the "intelligent native" is equally complaisant. The "farmer" and "native," therefore, are peculiarly "infallible."

It is wonderful how effective such an appeal is, even with men who ought to be able to see into the trick. If one wishes to wrest from the letter of Scripture some crotchet of his own, or if he wishes to show that Scripture contradicts itself, there is no better plan than to submit the question to some man of "plain common sense." It flatters one to think that "common sense" is a monopoly of his own: where Popes have erred, and Councils have proved fallible, and Doctors have disagreed, your "common-sense" man sees intuitively into the whole matter. With this unction laid to his soul, his mind reflects, as a polished mirror, whatever is brought before it. If you want "a weasel,"* a weasel forthwith appears. If you prefer "a whale," your "common-sense" man will swallow the largest whale you can bring him, and will even imagine it to be a "common-sense" whale. Hence, the infidel and the bigot appeal vehemently to common sense.

But Bishop Colenso appeals chiefly to that variety of the common-sense man, which he somewhat vaguely describes as the "intelligent Englishman;" and quotes

---

* Hamlet, Act III. Scene ii.

(Preface, p. 17) with approbation the "one great characteristic" of this class, to wit: that they are accustomed "*to seek for matter-of-fact truth in the first place*," and to delight in the "*practical element.*"

Now, in answering Bishop Colenso, I am bound, in some measure, to follow him into the court which he has chosen. Like him, I must appeal to "common sense," to "matter-of-fact," to the "practical element" which enters so largely into the minds of Englishmen and Americans. I only ask that "common sense" be not confounded with ignorant prejudice; that "matter-of-fact" be subordinated to Truth; that the "practical element," in a question of *spiritual* concern, be not so interpreted as to mean mere secularism.

The Bible is preëminently a large-minded Book. I ask, that its "difficulties" be dealt with in a large-minded way.

I will illustrate my meaning by considering, in the next chapter, some of Bishop Colenso's "difficulties."

V.

MOSES AND JOSHUA ADDRESSING ALL ISRAEL— EIGHT CHAPTERS OF DIFFICULTIES.

I. It is said in Deuteronomy i. 1 and v. 1, and Joshua viii. 34, 35, that "Moses spake unto *all* Israel: he called *all* Israel and said unto them." So likewise Joshua "read *all* the words of the Law .... *there was not a word* .... *which Joshua read not* before *all* the congregation .... with the women, and the little ones, and the strangers that were conversant among them."

Well: Bishop Colenso shows, and I feel no call to question his argument or to quote it, that it was physically *impossible* for *one* man to read *all* those words so as to be heard by *all* those people.

What then? Does the writer tell a lie? The Bishop acquits him of that charge. Does he commit a gross blunder? The Bishop thinks he does.

Now, were the sacred writer alive, to be cross-questioned on the subject, he might well begin his answer with the emphatic *Thou fool!* of another inspired penman. For who is so stupid as not to know, that phrases of the kind objected to are common to all languages, and are always understood in a conventional sense? A general draws up his *whole army:* does any one imagine that *he* draws up the whole? I utter my solemn opinion in the face of *the whole world:* do I expect the whole world to stand and look at me? St. Paul, publicly in Church, and privately from house to house, declared to his converts *the whole counsel of God:* did he deliver an exhaustive treatise on theology to every Christian family? Our Lord said to His Apostles, " Go ye into *all the world*, and preach the Gospel to *every creature:* " was there ever a man silly enough to suppose that He intended all the Apostles actually to preach to every creature, alive or dead, animal, vegetable, or mineral, on the face of *the whole earth*? On the Day of Pentecost, devout Jews came up to Jerusalem out of *every nation under Heaven:* do we understand from this that even a tenth of the nations were literally represented?

An " intelligent Englishman " may be " matter-of-fact " enough to boggle at such phrases. An intelligent American cannot possibly mistake them. For, every four years, the President of the United States stands on the East Porch of the Capitol, and delivers an " inaugural address "—and generally a pretty long one—to the *whole country,* with perhaps some incidental remarks to all mankind. What seems " impossible," therefore, to Bishop Colenso, we regard as an easy and natural proceeding. And even an " intelligent Englishman," I dare say, may meet occasionally with a public document beginning in terms like these —" Know *all men* by these presents : " if so, he will readily enough understand that the *literal* meaning of words is often a thing quite different from the sense which they really bear.

But it seems like trifling to argue on such a point. It will be enough to remind the reader of Bishop Colenso's book, that the whole of Chapter V. rests solely for its support upon such verbal cavilling as that which I have exposed.

II. The same is true of Chapter IV. wherein the author shows, by an arithmetical calculation, that the Court of the Tabernacle *could not possibly have accommodated* the Congregation of Israel; and consequently that the command (Levit. viii. 1–4) to "gather the Congregation together unto the door of the Tabernacle," and the assertion that "the assembly was gathered unto the door," are both absurdities.

The first "absurdity" is common enough among matter-of-fact Americans. We often see that great Behemoth, "the Public," invited to places, into which no effort could squeeze the thousandth part of his huge person. And even in Church matters, things of the same sort occur. A notice is often read in our city Churches, announcing some special service in one place or another, and adding, "This Congregation is respectfully requested to attend." Now, considering that the invitation is given simultaneously to some fifty congregations, and that the place to which they are invited would be crowded to suffocation if any three of them were to attend, we may judge how absurd such a notice would be in the eyes of Bishop Colenso.

The second "absurdity" needs no such parallels: for it is so worded as to give no handle to word-catchers, however eager they may be. It merely says that "the assembly"—however great or small—"was gathered *unto* the door:" a phrase which aptly enough describes the appearance of a great gathering—whether a " mass meeting " in this country or a religious jubilee in the East—when the place at which they assemble is too strait for them. The Caaba, which to this day is the shrine of the whole Moslem world, is an edifice of extremely scant dimensions. Yet the immense crowds which resort there annually manage in some way to " gather unto the door."

III. Again, in Chapter VI : " The extent of the Camp, compared with the Priest's duties, and the daily necessities of the people," is in Bishop Colenso's eyes another egregious blunder : because *the Priest* is commanded (Levit. iv. 11, 12) to " carry " all refuse " without the camp " and to burn it.*

The Bishop evidently supposes that, if a man should take a contract to clean the streets of New York, he is bound thereby to take broom and shovel in hand, and do the whole work himself. Possibly, if the contract were made in English, a matter-of-fact Jury, with a Colenso to prosecute and a Shylock to expound the law, might so interpret his bond. But the Hebrew Priest was secured against such a mishap by the fact, strangely overlooked by Bishop Colenso, that the command to *carry forth and burn* is expressed in the *causative* mood : literally, he shall " cause to go forth " —a distinction that would have saved him in the eyes of Shylock, who knew something of Hebrew, if not in those of Bishop Colenso.

IV. The difficulty in Chapter XXI. is somewhat greater, though evidently of the same character. The Priests were obliged (2 Chron. xxx. 16, xxxv. 11) to

---

* I forbear quoting, or answering, the vile jokes of the Bishop about the sanatory regulation in Deut. xxiii. 14. The context, verse 9, shows that it was meant for the *military* camp.

sprinkle the blood of the lambs slain for the Passover; also (Levit. xvii. 2–6) to *sprinkle the blood* of every ox, or lamb, or goat, slain by any of the people for sacrifice: which slaying, moreover, was to be done " at the door of the Tabernacle." In the same way, in Chapter XX, the numerous minute *duties* of the Priests (Levit. i.–vi., xii.–xv., xxviii., xxix.) and the *provision* made for their support (Num. xviii. 9–11, 14–18, &c.) were *enormously* disproportioned to *the number* of the Priests; that is, supposing the number of Priests and People to have been precisely that which appears on the face of the narrative.

This last supposition is open to discussion: for the present, however, I assume it to be true.

Now, as to the nicer points involved in this controversy,* they have been discussed by Kurtz and other learned commentators, times without number; and it has been abundantly shown that on a liberal construction the difficulties may be explained. As my object is merely to expose the general fallacy which underlies the cavils of Bishop Colenso, I pass by these *minutiæ;* and content myself with calling attention to a few obvious considerations.

The Law, as given by the hand of Moses, was necessarily prospective: being intended, not for the forty years of wilderness-life merely, but for a long period beyond, to the coming of the Messiah. This being the case, it necessarily contained enactments which could go into force only as circumstances admitted. The maxim, *necessitas non habet legem,* is so self-

---

* For example, Whether the Priesthood, which pertained to all the " nation of Priests," was suddenly confined in all particulars to Aaron and his sons, or was *gradually* transferred.

evident to man, that no law however precise can be supposed to abrogate it, and no man of common sense can doubt the lawfulness of its application, when the necessity really exists.

Hence, with regard to *the duties* of the Priests. If these duties were, in the wilderness, disproportioned to their strength, the Priests had sense enough, and Moses had sense enough, to perform them so far as they were able, leaving the rest to be performed as their ability increased. So, with regard to the *provision of food* made for them in the Law : doubtless, they ate as much as they wanted ; and if anything remained over, Moses was present, a living interpreter of the Law, who could readily suggest to them what to do with the rest. And that there actually was some such power of adaptation to circumstances, is shown by the fact (Josh. v. 6, 7) that for *forty years* the essential rite of *circumcision* was universally neglected. But if Moses could permit so glaring an irregularity as that, we may be sure that he had some way of suspending, or adapting, other enactments of the Law.

A Bishop, in confirming, is strictly required by *rubric*, to *lay his hands upon the head of every one severally, saying,* &c. What can be more explicit? Yet what Bishop, if he has a large number to be confirmed, ever troubles himself with the letter of such a rubric? The Apostles, in like manner, were commanded to preach to every creature, *baptizing* and *teaching* all. Yet St. Paul, the most active of the Apostles and the least likely to decline any portion of his duties, thanked God that *he* had baptized none of his Corinthian converts. It is well for him that he has not fallen into the hands of Bishop Colenso. But the Bishop may catch him yet, when he comes—as he promises—to the examination of the New Testament.

But the Law, it may be urged—and Bishop Colenso fails not to urge it—required obedience in *every* point. So it did. And so does all law: the moral law requires it, as much as the ceremonial; the Christian law, as much as the Judaic. " Whosoever shall keep the whole law and yet offend in *one* point, he is guilty of all ? " But what is the inference from this ? Simply, that law—as such—is far beyond the ability of man to meet. It is a measure of his shortcomings, not of his performances. It convicts him of sin: it does not assure him of righteousness. It kills, but does not quicken. Now, if God, in giving a ceremonial law to the Jews, introduced into it that feature which pervades all law; if He gave ordinances of perfection, far beyond the practical reach of any man or class of men: it merely proves that He was consistent with Himself; that He did not intend to give flesh *the glory* of fulfilling—even in the smallest matters—the fulness of His requirements.

The more clearly it is proved, therefore, that the Law, as given by Moses, presented a standard impossible of attainment, the more fully is Moses shown to be in harmony with St. Paul.

But this is beyond the depth of such critics as Bishop Colenso. He is content to stand on plain "matter-of-fact:" with broad views of the Divine purpose he will not trouble himself. Well, then: as a mere matter-of-fact, the same writer who gives us the strict *minutiæ* of the Law informs us continually, in the same narrative, that the Law was very indifferently observed. In great matters and small, the Jews were perpetually transgressing. Even Moses (Exod. iv. 24-26) was astonishingly negligent, in some points. If this be so, it is plain that the writer of the Pentateuch never intended it to be supposed that the law given by him was literally enforced in the wilderness; consequently, all argument based upon the difficulties of its observance either goes for nothing, or else proves (what we knew before) that it was imperfectly carried out.

V. In Chapter XXII, the Bishop finds out by calculation a chronological difficulty.

The death of Aaron being mentioned in Num. xx. 29, the narrative goes on with a variety of other events summarily related, coupled (as is common in Bible history) by the copulative "and."

"They mourned for Aaron thirty days."

"*And* when king Arad the Canaanite, which dwelt in the south, heard tell that Israel came by the way of the spies, *then* he fought against Israel."

The Bishop conveniently puts "*after this*" for "and," thereby assuming that the events connected with king Arad were strictly *after* the mourning for Aaron, whereas they may have been simultaneous with it, or partly before and partly after—nothing being more common in history than this gathering up, as it were, of facts which overlap one another in point of time.

But the Bishop, having assumed this strictly consecutive character of the events named, arbitrarily allows *a month* for their transaction.

So with the events that follow: he makes them all strictly consecutive. For example, when "Moses *sent to spy out* Jazer, and they took the villages thereof, and drove out the Amorites that were there" (Num. xxi.

32), the natural supposition would be, that said event was what we would call in modern parlance *a detached expedition*, which might be doing its work while the main body of the people were engaged in other affairs. But the Bishop assumes it to be a work of the whole people, and allows for it a *fortnight* more.

And so he goes on, *assuming* in each case that the events related followed each other like mules along a mountain path, the head of the one tied fast to the tail of the other, and *allowing* for each a fortnight, month, or whatever else he chooses; and having thus dictated his sum in arithmetic, invites us to " add up."

I beg to be excused. Events in history are not tied to each other's tails, in such a fashion as that. The word " and " in historical writers does not mean " after this." A detached movement in an army is not consecutive to the main movement; it is more often simultaneous with it.

And especially in early writers: any one who has studied the style of the old historians, or even of historians so modern comparatively as the four Evangelists, knows that the copulative " and " is in itself no guide to the order of the things narrated. Such writers, it is well known, are negligent of chronology, unless there happens to be need of exactness in that respect. And when there is need, and they wish to be exact, they generally signify it by such definite phrases as " then," " after this," " about this time," or the like. The Bishop's assumptions, therefore, are purely gratuitous. To add up " the sum " which he bases upon them may be good exercise for an infant-school, but to one who knows his right hand from his left, it would be idle in the extreme.

But the Bishop thinks otherwise. His six or seven *assumptions* being duly added to about the same number of *allowances*, and no assumptions or allowances being credited to the other side—for the Bishop's arithmetic admits no rule of subtraction—he finds the sum-total to be a greater amount of work done than could possibly have been done in the "six months" which Moses has allotted to it.

VI. One or two more examples will suffice for the present chapter. In Chapter VIII. of the Bishop's work, "the Israelites dwelling *in tents*," and in Chapter IX, "the Israelites *armed*," are to be regarded as manifest slips, on the part of Moses, because, by Colenso's arithmetic, it appears *impossible* to have gotten tents or arms for *all* the people. Especially was this impossible, because (the Bishop decrees) their tents *must* have been of "skins," and their arms must have been—the Bishop does not say what. Besides, how could they get beasts enough to carry all this baggage?

Perhaps the beasts they had, carried their own skins for awhile: a thrifty arrangement, which would go far toward meeting *three* of the Bishop's difficulties. It would provide materials for tents, when the beasts should be slain; it would be an inducement to slay most of the beasts at as early a date as possible, thus meeting incidentally another difficulty of the Bishop, Chapter XII—namely, that of finding food in the wilderness for so many cattle; it would feed the people in the interval before the *manna* was sent. And as to *arms*, a hardy people, engaged in making bricks, are never without weapons of some sort or other.

But, apart from considerations of this kind, where

does Moses say that *all* the Israelites had the comfort of tents? From what does the Bishop infer that *all* the tents were of "skins." Moses says (Exod. xvi. 16), "Take ye every man for them which are in his tents." But this no more implies that every man had tents, and especially skin tents, than the phrase, "Take ye every man for them which are in his house," would imply that every man had a house, and that a brick house. The Israelites, in all probability, were very indifferently provided with domestic comforts. As a people just escaped from bondage and hard labor, they would need but little in that way. And that they had but little, we may infer from their oft-repeated wish to go back into Egypt.

VII. The same general remark applies to the difficulty of Chapter XII, namely, that of finding food for "the sheep and cattle in the wilderness." That the Israelites were hard put to it, at times, the narrative plainly enough declares. There is no necessity, however, for making so hard a case of it as Bishop Colenso does. The wilderness, at that time, was doubtless a desert in many parts: but not necessarily so much of a desert as it is at the present day. As compared with Egypt on the one side, and Canaan on the other, it may have been quite sterile. But, as Egypt now is a desert, compared with Egypt then; or as Canaan now is a desert, compared with Canaan then; so also it may be with the wilderness between. Though a "desert" in ancient times, it may have been vastly less of a desert than it is just now. The difficulty, therefore, though it was undoubtedly great enough to be seriously felt, was by no means insuperable.

But, in all these cases, covering some eight chapters

of Bishop Colenso's book, the difficulty—save with regard to the *precise number* of the people, which I reserve for special consideration—is occasioned almost solely by a "matter-of-fact" determination, to treat the Pentateuch as one would treat a sum in arithmetic. Hence no allowance is to be made for idioms, conventional phrases, and the like; none, for such omissions of mere details as are common to all writers. The bald and naked letter, as it is in English, interpreted by English matter-of-fact sense as exhibited in Bishop Colenso, is to be pressed to the utmost against the narrative of Moses; and no hypothesis, no supplying of probable details, no allowance for the peculiarities of ancient times, no faith in that Omnipotence which led the people, is to be admitted in its favor.

Hypothesis, however, is to be excluded, only when it may serve to clear up the meaning of Moses: should it help to confound his meaning, the Bishop not only freely admits it, but gives it a quasi-infallibility by a liberal use of the word *must*. Where other writers would say, It *may* have been so and so, Bishop Colenso prefers to say, It *must* have been.

And it is also to be noted, that no reference is to be made to the hundreds of minute touches, showing a personal familiarity with Egyptian and desert life, which to minds of the highest order have demonstrated the historical character of the Pentateuch. Bishop Colenso has no notion of "a balance" of probabilities. If he can prove ten points against Moses, the hundred points in his favor need not be alluded to. In short, as I have said before, the Bishop's arithmetic is all addition, and no subtraction: he keeps a ledger, in which all the columns are *debit*, and none *credit*.

AN APOLOGY TO GOOD CHRISTIANS FOR "THINGS NEW AND OLD."

But here I foresee a possible objection, coming from a quarter for which I have great respect.

Some good Christian may say : " Are you not conceding *too much* to these conventional, or idiomatic phrases? If you grant that the words 'all' and 'every' and 'every . . . under heaven,' and the like, express ideas so much more limited than one at first sight would think possible, may you not be forced into dangerous interpretations of other passages than those which you have so far quoted?"

I answer, There is a danger. And I can see the application to some passages—for example, the Mosaic account of the Deluge—which, for one, I like to receive in the sense that has been commonly given to them.

Still, Interpretation is a science that must grow with other sciences. While its principles are always the same, the applications of those principles are continually enlarging with the lapse of time; because the horizon of human thought is continually enlarging. In the days of the Apostles, the *world*—the *oikoumene*—the *habitat* of man—was virtually little more than the Roman Empire. In the days of Moses, it was a space still more contracted. At the present day it embraces both sides of the globe. From the Divine point-of-view, this is a fact of little importance. God contemplates the part in the whole, and the whole in any part. He sees in the mustard-seed the full mustard-tree. And as with God, so with the sacred language inspired by God. Its words are "spirit and life," in more senses than one. They are germinating words, words that bear fruit for one age with seeds of other fruits for ages to come after. The interpretation that may answer for to-day, because it is large enough to fill the mind of to-day, may expand to-morrow, in order to fill up the mind of to-morrow. Thus Interpretation may grow, though it may not change. Its principles being fixed, in the laws of human speech, and its form being determined, in the Faith once delivered to the Saints, and its stand-point established, in the Church, the Pillar and Ground of Truth, it may go on for the future, as it has gone on in the past, re-adjusting itself from time to time, while remaining in all essentials continually the same.

Thus, it has adjusted itself already to the Copernican system of Astronomy: if other systems of science should prove equally true, it may with equal safety to the Scriptures adjust itself to them.

Hence, while I acknowledge some danger in any explanations that may seem to threaten a received view of difficult passages in Scripture, yet I am confident that the danger is less than is imagined. And to those, who abide by the Church, and plant their feet on that Rock on which the Church is built, there is no danger whatsoever. If others are in danger, it is because they despise the safeguards of Faith which God in His goodness hath provided.

At all events, the allowance we have to make for the force of idioms involves no concession of the Divine word itself. It involves only a closer study of the laws of human speech. Those laws, if examined, may enable us, in the work of harmonizing religion and science, to go further than at first we might think it possible to go. If so, let us follow those laws.

I may add that a real belief in Inspiration, as in the full sense Divine, almost necessarily *implies* a progressive interpretation. The Holy Ghost speaks *in* and *through* an age, using the idioms of that age, but not *for* that age alone through which He speaks. Hence, while Interpretation as a whole is fixed, being nothing more or less than the Creed or Rule of Faith, the interpretation of particular parts of Scripture may wonderfully develop. Thus, a thousand years ago, no one thought of the heavenly lights as other than fiery spangles; and therefore no one cared whether they were "set in the firmament" the first day or the fourth. Consequently, no one troubled himself much about the precise words of Moses on the subject. Now the case is different. We have learned to study the stars more closely: consequently, we study more closely what the Divine word has to say about them. The result is that we find out something previously overlooked. Where Moses speaks of "lights," we notice that the word (in Hebrew) means more accurately "light-holders"—a term that harmonizes more fitly with the latest results of Science.

Thus Science acts upon Interpretation, as the sunlight acts upon a writing in invisible ink. It does not create a new meaning: it merely brings out to view a hitherto hidden meaning.

"There is nothing hid which shall not be manifested; neither was anything kept secret, but that it should come abroad." Science is fulfilling this prophecy, in reference to the secrets of Nature. Every year, a prejudice is dispelled: every year something hidden for ages comes out into the light. Why may we not expect the same, in reference to things which have been "hid" in the letter of the Scriptures? Why can we not allow that much may have been kept secret, by being couched in idiomatic language, with the *intention* that ultimately it should come abroad? Discoveries result, either from shedding some new light upon a well-known subject, or else from contemplating the subject from a new point-of-view. Now Science undoubtedly sheds new lights. It unquestionably puts us in new points-of-view. May not this lead to new interpretations of the Bible, even as it has led to new interpretations of Nature? It must, if interpreters are alive to the demands of their sacred calling. For "a scribe instructed unto the kingdom of Heaven is like a householder that bringeth forth out of his treasure things new and old."

In fact, there is an essential difference between our Faith, which rests upon the sense of Scripture as a whole, and what we properly call our "views" of particular passages of Scripture.

The latter may be enlarged, or modified, or rendered more clear, or may even in some cases be materially changed, without in the slightest degree affecting the former.

And as with our views of certain texts, so also with our views of the nature of Inspiration. Most persons start with the matter-of-fact idea, that the soul of the inspired person is, like a soul possessed, merely a passive instrument in the Hand of the Inspirer. The early Church exploded that idea. The man inspired remains every whit a man. He is, in fact, a man intensified. And inspired writings, too, are preëminently human writings. There is in the Bible more flesh and blood, if I may so speak, than in any other extant literature.

It is proper, therefore, to be cautious, not only with regard to *new* views of Scripture texts, but also with regard to old views. For if a new view to-day is suggested in part by the science of to-day, the old view of yesterday may equally have been suggested by the science of yesterday. The only safe rule is to use the eyes that God hath given us, in the light that He vouchsafes, and from that stand-point of the Church which He hath provided for us.

I make these remarks, not for Bishop Colenso, but with a view to critics of a much nobler type. Many of these feel that Interpretation is cramped, and their own hands tied, and an open field left to the infidel assailant, by the timorousness of those who mistake a popular sense of Scripture for the Scripture itself; and who therefore start at everything that disturbs popular ideas. A true faith in the Bible admits no such alarms.

VII.

JACOB'S FAMILY LIST.

Bishop Colenso devotes his second and third chapters to supposed errors in the List of the *Seventy Souls* who went *with Jacob* into Egypt.

There are four names on the List (Gen. xlvi. 12, 17) which were evidently inserted *after* Jacob's arrival in Egypt: *evidently* inserted, because it is obvious* that the persons named, being grand-children of Judah and Asher, could not have been in existence before that event: *Colenso*, p. 61.

The matter has puzzled the interpreters, and various devices for disentangling the knot have been learnedly suggested. Bishop Colenso manages to make sport of these devices, and by some twist of his own seems to get the whole affair into a worse tangle than ever.

The *fact*, fairly stated from Scripture, is simply this:

Jacob's Family List, whether written in any way or merely committed to memory, contained before he went into Egypt precisely *seventy* souls: though *four* of these, namely his two wives† and two of the sons of Judah,‡ were *souls of the departed*. Thus, arithme-

---
* I concede this point: though good critics have disputed it.
† Gen. xlviii. 7; xlix. 31.   ‡ Gen. xxxviii. 7, 10.

tically, and in a matter-of-fact way, Jacob had *sixty-six* in his company when he first settled in Egypt: but religiously, or as some might say poetically,—in the spirit of the little maid of Wordsworth's ballad, who insisted so strenuously, " We are seven,"—he might still count them seventy.

To this fact may be added the following *probabilities*.

When Jacob arrived in Egypt, he probably gave to his List the title or heading which it still bears—namely, *the Names of the Children of Israel which came with him into Egypt:* Exod. i. 1: Gen. xlvi. 8–28. And it is likely enough that he did this, without troubling himself to erase, either from his tablets or his memory, the names of the dear departed souls whom the kind-hearted and faithful Patriarch still regarded as " of his company."

At a later date, however, he may have revised his List. Affectionate heads of families are apt to do such things. Their Family List is the solace of their old age: and they turn it over and over, as fondly as a miser counts over his hoarded money. The Patriarch, then, turning his List over in this way, and counting his seventy souls which the Lord had given him, and reluctant to erase his four departed souls, availed himself of the first opportunity to substitute for them four new souls—among his great-grandchildren—whom the Lord in His goodness had granted him *in their place.** Thus the names of the grandchildren of Judah and Asher may easily have come in. No other names were added, because no others were needed.

---

* Gen. xxx. 9, &c., shows that the idea of *substitution* could go much further then, than would be considered proper now.

The mystic force of the number *seventy*—a well-known sacred number—may have stimulated his desire to keep his List up to that figure, after it had once reached it. If he had been a matter-of-fact man, the desire of keeping to a round number might also have had something to do with it. For arithmetic, among the Ancients, was very loosely taught. No Colensos then had put forth text-books on the subject. Moreover, there was not much *writing* done in those primitive times. Men carried their note-books in their brains, rather than in their pockets. It will be readily seen, then, that a certain preference for round numbers was the most natural thing in the world.

However all this may be, Moses took the Family List of Jacob, just as Jacob had left it; and inserted it —with all its sins against arithmetic on its head—in his books of Genesis and Exodus.

But, as an *inspired* man, had he a right to overlook or to sanction these sins against modern arithmetic?

I answer, Yes: the Holy Ghost did not inspire him to be a pedant, or arithmetician. He was raised up, and inspired, for a holier and better work. As a historian of Truth, and not a detailer of mere facts,—as a Prophet of the old world, not a Gradgrind of the nineteenth century,—he concerned himself chiefly with weightier matters of the law.

If a slight inaccuracy in figures—an inaccuracy, that is, from *one* point-of-view—should turn out to be the means of suggesting spiritual reflections, it would be just the kind of inaccuracy that large-minded men of all ages delight in: an inaccuracy, I may reverently add, not alien or displeasing to the Spirit of Divine Truth.

And even Bishop Colenso is obliged to grant, that *some* inaccuracies of the narrative can be explained, by allowing for primitive modes of expression and of thought. Thus Jacob himself is included among his own sons (Gen. xlvi. 8), and among the sons of Leah (ver. 12)—see Colenso, p. 67. But, if some inaccuracies of this kind are manifestly idioms, resulting from habits of thought impossible to us, why may not the other inaccuracies result from similar, though less obvious, peculiarities?

But his lordship is so reluctant to concede anything in that way, further than he is absolutely forced to it, that to avoid it he commits a slight, but very suspicious, inaccuracy himself. He speaks of Leah " and the other *wives* of Jacob " (p. 67) as being omitted because they were *dead*. Had he said, the other *wife*, the statement would have been strictly accurate (for the maids of Rachel and Leah were *in loco uxorum*, not wives in the proper sense), and would have gone far toward meeting one of his difficulties. Namely, he rejects the explanation that two of the four great-grandchildren *may* have been adopted as substitutes for the two deceased sons of Judah, by triumphantly asking, How do we account for the insertion of the other two? " If Hezron and Hamul are substituted for Er and Onan, *for whom* are *Heber and Malchiel* .... xlvi. 17, supposed to be substituted?" Now, supposing that Jacob had *two* wives deceased, the answer would be easy. Therefore, it is convenient to Bishop Colenso to speak as if Jacob had more than two wives. In short, he continually asks the question, If *four* names of persons born after the arrival in Egypt were inserted in the List, why not *more* than four? But he shuffles so as to conceal the obvious reply, that there were but four deceased persons, and consequently four substitutes were all that were needed.

There are like instances of unfairness all through the discussion. I omit them, because I do not care to accumulate mere points. I have shown that the peculiarities of Jacob's List *may* be accounted for. To attempt more, in so ancient a document, cannot be reasonably expected.

I may add that, in giving an explanation somewhat different from that of Hävernick, Hengstenberg, and other learned authorities, I do not intend in any way to disparage *their* solutions. I have preferred my own, merely because it was easier for me to express. A knot may be untied in a variety of ways. The best way of untying it, time and many minds alone can determine.*

Besides: the more ways there are of meeting a difficulty in Scripture, the more proof there is that the difficulty was intended, and provided for, in the general plan of Inspiration. It is not God's way to save us absolutely from temptation: it is rather, with the temptation, to open a way for our escape. One way of befriending men would be to allow no diseases. Another way would be to allow diseases, but alongside of them to provide sufficient remedies. Providence, on the whole, prefers the latter plan. We have no ground for supposing that Divine Inspiration would act otherwise, in principle, than as Divine Providence has done.

* Kennicott, Skinner and others have *almost* demonstrated, from Gen. xxxi. 38, 41, that Jacob served Laban *two* periods of twenty years each. If this be admitted,—and the original text seems to favor it,—all the difficulties connected with the chronology of Jacob's life disappear at once: see Kennicott's *Remarks*, &c.: or, Barrett's *Synopsis*.

VIII.

A FEW OTHER DIFFICULTIES.

Bishop Colenso has, undoubtedly, *one* real difficulty: namely, the number of the Israelites who went forth out of Egypt. But to give effect to this, he puts it at the head of a squad of supernumeraries; which, like a skilful scene-shifter, he manages to bring out again and again, so as to give them the appearance of a formidable host.

Some of these supernumeraries I have already considered. I must dispose of the rest, before coming to the one which gives them whatever importance they may seem to possess.

As in the cases noticed before, the difficulty lies mainly in that cavilling adherence to the bald and naked letter, that treatment of words as if they were mere counters, that way of spelling out a meaning with the eyes and fingers instead of reading it by the light of a sympathetic mind, which is pardonable (perhaps) in persons ignorant of letters, but which in a Scholar and a Bishop is without excuse. Interpret the whole Bible in this way, and the sacred Book becomes simply ridiculous. Interpret any literature in this way, and it becomes unintelligible jargon. But no writer expects to be treated in that way. The rough saying of Dr. Johnson, " Sir, I am bound to furnish you arguments, not brains,"—" *intelligibilia præbeo, non intellectum*" —is a sort of implied contract between the writer and the reader, which none but the veriest pedant will fail to respect.

And there is the less excuse for this kind of pedantry in dealing with the Bible, because the sacred Book condemns it, and warns against it, and in the plainest terms shows up its stupidity and folly. For example, the words of wisdom " are all plain *to him that understandeth;*" but, " like lame legs that will not dance," * " like a thorn in a drunkard's hand," " so is a parable in the mouth of fools : " see Proverbs xxvi. 7, 9. And our Lord, in the New Testament, confuting the wretched literalness of the Pharisees, invariably rebukes them as " fools and blind." So also the warning of St. Paul, " Not the letter, but the spirit." In which and numberless other passages, in the Old Testament and the New, the necessity of *intelligent* interpretation, as opposed to the merely literal and pedantic, is so manifestly laid down that no candid mind can miss it.

But to come to the " difficulties : "

(1.) " And Moses said, Thus saith the Lord, About *midnight* will I go out into the midst of Egypt : " &c., Exod. xi. 4–8.

(2.) " *And he went out from Pharaoh* in great anger : " xi. 8.

(3.) " *And the Lord spake* unto Moses and Aaron in the land of Egypt, saying, This month shall be unto

* Literally, "the legs of the lame are not equal."

you, &c. . . . . Speak ye unto all the congregation of Israel, saying, In *the tenth day of this month* they shall take unto them every man a lamb . . . . . for a house . . . . . and ye shall keep it *unto the fourteenth day,*" &c., xii. 1–11.

(4.) "For I will pass through the land of Egypt *this night,*" &c., xii. 12.

Now these four passages, running consecutively and coupled by the word "and," might be understood to describe events following upon one another in the precise order given. If we strain the word *and*, they must be so understood. But, if so understood, they make downright nonsense. The writer would seem to say, that Moses, after predicting an event which was to take place the night immediately following, (1), *then* commanded the people to spend *four days* at least in preparing for that event, (3), and *then* added (4) that the event was to take place immediately that same night.

Such is the meaning if we press to the utmost the word *midnight* in the first passage, the word *and* in the second and third, and the word *this* in the fourth.

Bishop Colenso does not hesitate so to press them. *About midnight*, he declares, *must* mean the midnight of that day on which Moses spake: *this night* must mean the same—and he brings in the Hebrew word to prove it. Therefore, though the context (3) manifestly implies an interval of at least four days, we must not allow Moses the benefit of his context, but must summarily conclude (on the strength of Bishop Colenso's grammar) that the writer could not remember his own mind from one sentence to another.

Now, whether the writer of Exodus was an inspired

man or not, all the world will grant that he was not a simpleton. But, if Bishop Colenso's argument in Chap. X. is good for anything, it proves him to have been stupid to a most extraordinary degree.

And, unfortunately, if we are to trust the Bishop, the lapse already described is but a small part of the stupidity involved. In the *twelve hours* or so, to which Moses is arithmetically pinned down, *all* the people are to receive their first intelligence of the contemplated march; *all* are to prepare their lambs—being instructed the meanwhile in the minutiæ of the Passover; *all* are to borrow jewels from their neighbors the Egyptians; *all* are to get themselves in readiness for a move; *all* are to start, with their flocks and herds, and wives and children, marching from Goshen to Rameses, and from Rameses to Succoth, all on a single day!

For, the Bishop says, "This is, *undoubtedly*, what the story in the book of Exodus requires us to believe." For which "*undoubtedly*" he refers us to Exod. xii. 31 –41,—" the children of Israel journeyed from Rameses to Succoth,"—and to ver. 51—" it came to pass *the self-same day* that the Lord did bring the children of Israel out of Egypt." But if the Bishop lays such stress on *the self-same day*, why not lay an equal stress upon the leading *out of Egypt?* For the people were not fairly " out of Egypt" till they had crossed the Red Sea. Why not prove, then, while we are about it, that from Goshen to Rameses, and from Rameses to Succoth, and from Succoth to the east shore of the Red Sea, was all accomplished in one day's march? To be sure, the context might disprove it, and common sense would revolt at it: but what is "context" or "common sense" against Bishop Colenso's grammar?

An ordinary reader knows that the Bible, like other history, is mind speaking to mind, and that when mind thus speaks to mind, many details are often left to the intelligence of the reader. An ordinary reader, therefore, does not scruple to allow for many things, not expressly stated in a condensed and rapid history. Thus, when Cæsar describes a great campaign in the words, "Veni, Vidi, Vici," we feel at liberty to supply much, which Cæsar does not express. "Veni" implies a long journey by sea and land; "Vidi" includes more than the use of a single pair of eyes; "Vici" brings up pictures of the toil and tug of war. If we treat Moses, as we would treat Cæsar, we should not scruple to fill up his narrative, in like manner, with suggestions of simple details which he may not have thought it worth while to record. Thus, if the people were to march out of Egypt in haste, it is likely that he took proper measures beforehand to organize* them for such a journey. If they were to sacrifice lambs, it is probable (and the narrative expressly says) he gave them notice in time. So with other points too numerous to mention. But Bishop Colenso has one answer to all such charitable suggestions. Shylock-like, he repeats, "It is not found in the bond." Thus Tischendorf supposes —and it does not seem to be a violent stretch of imagination—that when the people travelled some *sixty* miles in *three* days, they took intervals of rest "between the three marching days." But Bishop Colenso allows no such daring hypothesis. "Nothing whatever *is said or implied* about these *days of rest*. There

---

* The Egyptians were splendid organizers; and their slaves were well accustomed to move rapidly in large bodies.

A FEW OTHER DIFFICULTIES. 67

would *surely* have been some reference made to them, if they really occurred." Thus the *probably* of Tischendorf is overwhelmed by the *surely* of Colenso. The object being to prove Moses a dunce, why should the game be spoiled by your charitable suppositions?

His remarks on the "War on Midian," Chap. XXII, bring out an objection of a higher kind: namely, *the cruelty* of destroying so many people. This objection is not new: and I answer, as it has always been answered, that the Midianites were destroyed, for their wickedness, by the command of God. It may be cruel in soldiers to extirpate a band of robbers. But if the soldiers are commanded so to do by legitimate authority, men regard it as an act of simple justice.

So also, the Bishop objects that the Lord accepted a tribute of "slaves" from among the captives, thus giving a sort of Divine sanction to the custom of holding slaves. That may be so. But if so, it merely proves that God did not consider "slavery" the worst thing that could happen to a man. Bishop Colenso may think otherwise. But his lordship's claims to infallibility are surely not superior to those of Moses or St. Paul.

I will not waste the time of the reader, by dwelling on the difficulties of Chapters XI, XII, XIII. They are precisely of the same character as those already discussed. The arguments employed—apart from that which rests on *the great number* of the Israelites—are invariably of the same arbitrary, technical, and hairsplitting description. If Moses is to be interpreted by Bishop Colenso's rules, we give up Moses, and with him we give up the best writers of all ages, as absolutely indefensible.

Indeed, I am not sure but that we shall be obliged, by the same rules of interpretation, to give up Bishop Colenso himself. For, on p. 224, in his "concluding remarks," he quotes as sound theology, "learned by the *direct teaching of the Spirit of God*," the following Hindoo maxim :

"*Whatsoever hath been made, God made.* Whatsoever is to be made, God will make. Whatsoever is, God maketh."

But if " God made whatsoever hath been made," He must have made among other things the Five Books of Moses. So that, after all, Bishop Colenso proves nothing against them by proving them " unhistorical." In fact, I never could understand why a Pantheist—and Bishop Colenso, on p. 224, fairly enrolls himself among that number—should object in any way to the Inspiration of the Scriptures, or should consider one part of the sacred volume more inspired than another. If " God is in all," why is He not in the Bible ? And if He is in the Bible, why object to the common belief in a Divine Inspiration ?

Nor is the Bishop quite consistent in his professed hostility to evasions, and in his devotion to matter-of-fact and literal interpretation.

Thus, in his Preface, he opposes the theory "that Noah's deluge was a *partial* one," partly on the ground that, " as waters must find their own level," a flood which covered the high hills in one part of the earth, must have covered the hills of the same height in other parts. He *ignores* the fact, that Hugh Miller and other advocates of the partial deluge theory suppose the flood to have been caused mainly by *a sinking* of that region which was overflowed : a supposition which, being an essential feature of the theory and answering the Bishop's objection, he was bound in common honesty to give.

There is even a worse lack of the plain dealing which he recommends, in his answer to the matter-of-fact objection, that our Lord Himself refers to Moses and evidently treats him and his writings as historical. This he evades by a very subtle distinction between His knowledge as God, and His ignorance as Man. As God, He knew Moses to be "unhistorical;" as Man, He knew nothing about it.

In the same way, because it suits the Bishop's purpose to do away with the most obvious meaning of St. Stephen's declaration in Acts vii. 6, he interprets the passage in precisely the same way that he calls "evasive," when it occurs in other writers. "At first sight .... it would *seem* that Abraham's descendants were to be *afflicted* for 400 years, in one land," &c. He then shows that the seeming meaning is not the correct one. His reasoning, in this instance, p. 153, is probably correct. But if he had reasoned the same way in all other instances, with similar allowance for the force of idioms, most of his difficulties would easily have been removed.

Again, he declares, p. 51, that "the notion of *miraculous or supernatural interferences* does not present to (his) mind the difficulties which it seems to present to some." Yet, if we appeal to *the Divine Power*, as solving the difficulties of the Exodus, the Bishop allows no force to anything of the sort.

A writer thus careless of his own consistency, and so subtle and evasive when it suits his purpose, would fare badly, if judged by the rigid rules which he applies to Moses.

IX.

SCRIPTURAL ARITHMETIC.

I COME now to what I have called the "one real difficulty" of Bishop Colenso's book.

It is the difficulty, and (perhaps) the impossibility of ascertaining the true number of the Israelites, at the time of the Exodus. The question with regard to it may be briefly summed up as follows:

While the number of the entire people is nowhere given, we are yet furnished with two kinds of *data*, from which it may be inferred. These *data*, however, seem intricate, confused, and not easily reconcilable with one another. I will proceed at once to the consideration of the *first* "kind," reserving the second to another chapter.

There are statements in numerals: as in Exod. xii. 37, which gives 600,000 men; Exod. xxxviii. 25–28, where there are 603,550, this sum being *checked* moreover by the tribute paid, namely 603,550 bekahs; Num. i. 46, where the number of each tribe is given, and all are added up to the sum of 603,550; Num. xxvi. 51, the last year in the wilderness, where again the tribes are given, and all come up to the amount of 601,730. These numbers stand for the fighting men.

But, on the other hand, the whole number of "firstborn, from a month old and upwards," which on statistical principles ought to be at least *one-fourth* of the entire male population, is in Num. iii. 43, computed at 22,273, not much more than *one-thirtieth* of the *adult* fighting men. This number also seems to be certified, *first*, by the purpose for which the census was taken, namely, that "all the first-born of the males" might be redeemed; *secondly*, by the exactness of the odd number, 273, which would indicate a count of the closest kind; *thirdly*, by the number of the Levites (Exod. iii. 39) substituted for the first-born, to wit, 22,000; and *fourthly* (Exod. iii. 46) by the special arrangement made for the 273 who could not find Levite substitutes.

Now, if we allow the adult males to be *one in four* of the population, and the "first-born" to be *one in seven*, we shall arrive at two quite different results. By the one, we shall get a population of about 2,500,000: by the other, of about 150,000.

To account for this difference, we may suppose the word "first-born" was used in some conventional sense, for a privileged class, and did not apply to *all* the eldest sons in the nation. It may have applied only to the eldest of certain families of purer blood: not to "the mixed multitude," Exod. xii. 38, which came out with them from Egypt. But this is only a guess; and other conjectures which have been framed seem hardly to cover the difficulty.*

If we could suppose, however, that "thousands" and "ten-thousands" were but vague expressions of multitude, like the word *legions* in the New Testament or *myriads* among the Greeks, the difficulty would be much diminished, if not absolutely done away. And

* See Appendix A.

there is much in the Scripture style to make such a supposition probable. Thus, when Moses speaks (Deut. xxxiii. 17) of "the ten-thousands of Ephraim and the thousands of Manasseh," we would infer at once, from the *modern* meaning of those numbers, that Ephraim was *ten times more* numerous than Manasseh: we find actually, however—according to that later census in Num. xxvi. 34, 37, which Moses had before him when he spoke—that Manasseh was by far the more numerous of the two. In the same way, in Num. x. 36, I find Moses speaking of the "*ten thousand thousands* of Israel:" an expression so Oriental, that our Version very properly reduces it to "the *many* thousands."

Such vagueness of expression leads one to suspect that when the census was taken (Num. i. 4, 16, &c.) *by the* "*heads of thousands*," these "thousands" of which they were "heads" may have been simply what we would call "regiments" or something of the kind: a "regiment" being the synonym of "a thousand" on the Army List, but not by any means necessarily containing that number of men. This suspicion is strengthened by the fact, that the "heads of thousands" are also described, in the same connection, as *heads of houses* or families: see ver. 4. But it is not probable that each "house" contained a round thousand, in the arithmetical sense of the word. It seems more probable, that it was counted for a thousand, in a purely conventional sense: so that the returns of the census were made in "thousands," or in "hundreds" corresponding to "companies," by the "heads of thousands" and "captains of hundreds," according to some rule known among themselves but not easily ascertainable in modern times.

SCRIPTURAL ARITHMETIC. 73

In short, the "tens" with their "captains of tens," the "hundreds" with their "captains of hundreds,"* the "thousands" with their "heads of thousands," may have been as indefinite, in respect of number, as *hamlets, villages, towns;* or *files, companies, regiments;* or any other words of acknowledged but vague division. The military language of our times may give some idea of the uncertainty of such expressions. But, it is probable, that our military system is much more exact—in a mathematical way—than was the *militia* system of Moses.

At all events, whatever theory we may adopt, there can be no doubt, that not only in the days of Moses, but for a long time after, all the round numbers were used in a most vague and bewildering manner. Thus, in the New Testament, where St. James (Acts xxi. 20) speaks of "thousands" of Jews, the original Greek uses the word "myriads:" that is, according to the Lexicons, "ten-thousands." So, in the Revelation, St. John sees in vision an army of *two hundred thousand thousand:* a phrase that would hardly have been used by the most daring poet, in an arithmetical age. In short, if we look into a Concordance for the word "thousand," we find a few places in which it *may possibly be* an exact expression of number; and even the word "ten-thousand" *may be* so understood in one or two instances: but in the great majority of cases, the meaning is so plainly vague, that to press the word mathematically seems little less than absurd.

---

* England, under king Alfred, had its "tithings" and "hundreds," presided over by a *decanus*, or *hundred-man*. Some of the "Hundreds" still remain.

4

But Bishop Colenso saves me the trouble of enlarging upon this view of the subject. After quoting a passage of Josephus, (p. 207, *note*,) in which that writer speaks of " many ten-thousands," at the same time referring to a previous statement where the number stands as " above 13,000," the critic goes on to add : " In fact, Josephus' numbers are very frequently as extravagant and unreal as those of the Scripture writers. . . . . It is impossible for us not to perceive that a systematic *habit* of exaggeration in respect of numbers prevails among Hebrew writers of history, probably from not realizing to their own minds the actual *meaning and magnitude* of the numbers employed."

The Bishop states the fact correctly, though invidiously, and hints at the probable explanation. Not only " the Hebrew writers," but all writers of antiquity; not only the " writers of history," but writers of every kind, had " a *habit* in respect of numbers," which, however, I will not call a " habit of exaggeration : " at least, not of exaggeration for any purpose of deception. It was more " probably " a habit of " not realizing to their own minds the *actual* meaning of numbers : " that is, the meaning in a *modern scientific* sense. In fact, they knew but little of arithmetic. Their counting and calculating was a slow and tedious and uncertain process. Men who have bound the ages by an intellectual spell, who still reign paramount in the world of thought, might have been gravelled by a simple sum in the Rule of Multiplication.* Hence a

---

* It has been doubted, on very good grounds, whether Homer's arithmetic extended beyond an hundred. It is certain, that he never added up his glorious catalogue of men and ships : or, if he

habit of mind and speech—for speech in all ages is but the image of mind:—which to us, at the present day, is well-nigh inexplicable. We see something like it, however, in every intelligent child. To such an one a round number is little more than a figure of speech. It stands for a vague idea which looms up in the imagination, but what the idea is, or what its numerical value, a "*non sine Diis animosus infans*" never troubles himself to ask.

Now the ancients, in some respects, were little better or worse than children. In the matter of numerals especially, they were, to use the language of the nineteenth century, "fanciful and puerile." A Pythagoras, a Plato, a St. Ambrose, a St. Augustine, could value numbers chiefly for the *mysteries* they contained: * and what cyphering they ever did was solely in pursuit of these sacred meanings. Now, can we appreciate

did, he found a *sum-total* which would have merited the birch in a modern children's school,—namely,

"Myriads as are the leaves and flowers in spring."

* As I refer more than once to this mystic treatment of numbers, I will give one example of it. St. Augustine, applying it to the 153 "great fishes" of John xxi. 11, says (in substance): *Seven* is "the gifts of the Spirit," *Ten* "the number of the commandments;" the two added together make *Seventeen*, the symbol of those who through the Spirit do His Commandments. "Now, add up"—and as soon as the Saint said this, the congregation immediately began to "add up," on their fingers—"all the numerals from *one* to *seventeen* inclusive, and you will find the sum to be *one hundred and fifty and three*. Therefore, 153 is the symbol of all who are to be saved from the beginning to the end of time." Examples of this kind abound in the Patristic writings; and there are few numbers, in the Old Testament or New, that were not subjected to this cabalistic treatment.

this? Can we by any effort enter into such a *habit* of mind?

It is hard, undoubtedly, to realize it to *our* minds: but to the ancients it was so real, that for them to conceive of numbers precisely as we do, would have been perhaps still harder.

At all events, the fact stares us in the face, that not the Hebrews only, as Bishop Colenso unfairly puts it, but the ancients generally, used numbers in a most inexplicable way. Who believes, at the present day, that the army of Xerxes numbered over a million? Who imagines that the chronology of the Egyptians, Hindoos or Chinese, was constructed on the rules of modern arithmetic? Who ever reads an ancient history without quietly putting the "sacred factor" *ten* under most of the figures in it?*

Bishop Colenso, then, is correct in speaking of the ancient practice in this way, as a sort of "habit." But what does that "habit" mean? It *may* mean that the ancients were prone to exaggerate. Or, it may mean simply, that numbers, and especially the high round numbers, have gradually undergone in process of time a change of value or meaning. Because a word remains in a language from age to age, it does not follow

---

* Lee, in his learned work on Inspiration, p. 365, similarly applies the factor 10 as a divisor of some of the round numbers in the Chronicles. He does it on the ground of probable corruptions in the text. The same divisor may be applied so widely to ancient numbers, that I am inclined to rest its application on a broader ground; and to suppose that *ten*—the symbol of infinity—was used very largely as a sacred multiple. Such a habit, puzzling as it is to modern times, may have been quite intelligible to contemporaries.

that its sense remains the same. The process by which a term assumes gradually a more exact and scientific meaning, is extremely difficult to trace. And especially is it difficult with regard to words of measure, or weight, or number. But most of all is it difficult, when we have to grope our way back through ages whose habits of mind are as different from ours, with regard to all matters of science, as the thoughts of an imaginative child from those of a pragmatic adult.

Besides this, numerals are more exposed, than other signs, to accidental corruptions, or intentional alterations. Nor is the frequent repetition of a number any absolute security against this danger. A corruption in one place may easily lead to an intended correction in another: and a later scribe may carry out the correction into all other places where he may fancy it to be needed. Especially might this take place, if the scribes should happen to be, as most of the ancients were, under the influence of some *mystic science* of numbers. This would give to their corrections a *systematic* appearance.

Besides this, again: if numbers were used so commonly in a vague, and perhaps mystic sense, we cannot be certain in all cases that the sacred writers themselves were inspired to go against the prevailing use, or to antedate the exactness of a later age. The Prophets certainly used mystic numbers. If the historians sometimes did the same, it would be natural at a time when "statistics" were little cared for; and might lessen the value of their writings so far as "statistics" are concerned; but would weigh nothing against their general historical character. On this point, however, I propose to speak more fully in another place.

Against such hypotheses of a vague or mystic use of numbers, or of corruptions of the numbers originally used, there seems to be one strong objection. In Exod. xxxviii. 25, 26, the number of the men is *checked* by a corresponding number of *bekahs*—the "bekah" being the offering of a man—contributed to the use of the Tabernacle. But, here again, the general principle applies. What a "thousand" meant, at so remote a period, when applied to "bekahs," may be as uncertain as when the same word is applied to men. A certain *weight* of bekahs, or a certain *measure*, may have counted as a "thousand." A "pound sterling," in English, might easily be imagined—especially at some remote period when the English shall be a dead language—to mean actually a "pound" of something now used as money. But whatever may have been its original use, it actually means something less than one-third of a pound. How far the same conventional use of words may have gone, in the days of Moses, especially of words relating to weight, or measure, or number, is a question by no means easy to settle. This much, however, may be safely said. *If* numbers were used at all in a conventional or mystic way, either by the original writers or by subsequent correctors of the Bible text, the use would be made to apply to the "bekahs," as well as to the "men," in the instance mentioned above: so that the question of the actual number would remain as open as ever.

It is certain enough, that not only the Pentateuch, but most of the books of the Bible, down to the Apocalypse, give evidence of a peculiar *habit*—a habit which to our minds is but vaguely intelligible—with regard to the use of numerals. And this habit, moreover, seems to have a method in it. The multiple *ten* seems to abound. Other sacred multiples, from 2 to 10,—for almost all the digits had well-known mystic values,—*seem* to be present in places where a modern reader would hardly think of looking for them. Thus, to take a few instances of the larger numbers: there are armies of Israelites, ranging from 307,500 to 400,000, and 580,000, and 800,000, and 1,000,000, and even 1,160,000 warriors; 2 Chron. xiii. 3 . . . . . . xvii. 14–19. In the same way (2 Chron. xiii. 17) "there fell down slain 500,000 chosen men." So, in other places, there are captives and spoils in the same stupendous proportions: all under circumstances, moreover, which would hardly seem to require one tenth of the number given. A few such instances are quoted by Bishop Colenso and other skeptics to bring the Bible into contempt. A few are quoted also by Lee and other defenders of the Bible, to show the probability of interpolations. I do not know that any one of recent writers has gone into the subject thoroughly, with a view to ascertain how far there is a *system* in the Bible numerals, or what that system is, or how far a fair application of it might furnish reliable *data* for the reduction of the ancient figures to modern statistical terms. The early Christian fathers assumed that there was a system in the sacred numerals. The best-known moderns have assumed the contrary. I doubt whether there has been any such thorough and methodical investigation, as would prove which of these assumptions is the better grounded.

Now, to bring the question to a point: In an essay like this, which aims to be as practical as the nature of the subject will allow, it is not necessary to show which of the *hypotheses* above suggested is most likely to be the true one. It will be enough to say, in a case of such acknowledged difficulty, that any one of them is far more reasonable, and far easier of belief, than the conclusions to which we are led by Bishop Colenso's reasoning.

For, if we are to credit him, the writer of the Pentateuch was so careful with regard to numbers, and so expert an arithmetician, as to *check* his principal statements with the most business-like precision. At the same time, he was so careless and inexpert, as to commit errors, frequent, palpable, astounding, beyond the power of the wildest imagination to conceive of, in a man of sense.

Thus, Chapter XVIII, " Dan, in the first generation, has *one* son," which in the fourth generation, Bishop Colenso shows, would amount to about " 27 warriors : " yet Moses gives him an increase of " 62,700 warriors." In the same way, " the 4 sons of Kohath increased in the *third* (Aaron's) generation to 8 : " yet (according to Bishop Colenso) the same writer who gives this moderate increase for three generations so multiplies the same family in the *fourth* (that is, *his own*) generation, that " 6 men must have had between them . . . . . . 2,748 sons, and we must suppose about the same number of daughters." And there are (according to Bishop Colenso) other like blunders of the same gigantic dimensions, all accompanied by plain matter-of-fact statements alongside of them in the text, which effectually expose their error.

Now the writer of the Pentateuch was undoubtedly a man of sense. Though he may not have been a statistician, in the modern sense of the word, yet he well knew the rate at which families increase in *one or two generations,* and his study and observation evidently lay much in that particular line. Could such a man, then, make such a blunder as that which Bishop Colenso exposes? Is it not more likely, that the Bishop has misunderstood him? May it not have been that Moses, like other historians, *omitted* many facts and names which, if instead of writing history he had been dictating a sum in arithmetic, he might have thought proper to mention?

Or, if this supposition will not answer, may it not be that, with regard to his use of numbers, there is something which is not understood by the modern mind: something which scholars and interpreters have as yet not thoroughly explored?

This last was, in the main, the position taken by Origen and other interpreters of the early Church. They reasoned that if a good writer is so interpreted as to commit him to an absurdity, the fault is more likely to be in *the mode of interpretation* than in the writer himself. Hence, as the alleged "absurdities" of Scripture are always found in a too *literal* rendering of idioms, phrases or numbers, these idioms and numbers should not be taken to the letter, except in cases where it can be shown that it was intended they should be so taken. From this maxim sprang that *mystic* interpretation of Scriptural numbers, so common among the Fathers.

Moderns are averse to the mystic science, and prefer the hypothesis of "corruptions" or "interpolations." The Hebrew letters which stand for numerals may be corrupted by a line or dot. Many of them, we know from the evidence of Manuscripts, have been so corrupted. Where there is a real discrepancy, then, either among the numbers themselves, or between the numbers and the general drift of the text, it is easier to suppose that Manuscripts have suffered in the lapse of ages,* than that a sensible writer, like Moses, should have committed an egregious blunder.

I think there is room for *all* these hypotheses: for, of the figures employed in Scripture, some are doubtless corrupt; some are vague; some are mystic: and to decide which is which in any given case requires all the tact and learning that Interpretation, as a science, can bring to bear on the subject.

How this admission affects the Pentateuch as a collection of *inspired* and *historical* books, I shall treat more precisely in the Chapter after the next.

* The differences among the Hebrew, Samaritan and Septuagint copies of the Scriptures, are most conspicuous in respect of numerals.

X.

FACTS BEARING ON THE NUMBER OF THE ISRAELITES.

I PROCEED to say a few words on the *second* kind of *data*, referred to in the beginning of the last Chapter: namely, the facts or statements bearing incidentally on the number of the Israelites, to be found here or there through the Pentateuch.

In Deut. vii. 7, Moses declares to the Israelites, that God did not choose them by reason of their number: "because," says he, "ye were the fewest of all people." In the same way, he pictures the people saying of the Canaanites, vii. 17, "These nations are more than I." In the same way again, vii. 22, the Canaanites were not to be consumed *at once*, lest the wild beasts should "increase upon" their destroyers. But, as Bishop Colenso shows, a population that could furnish 600,000 warriors could not be considered either few or weak, or insufficient to expel the beasts, in so small a country as Palestine.

To this, Bishop Colenso adds a number of facts, which he grossly exaggerates: such as "the size of the Tabernacle compared with the number of the Congregation," and other things of the same sort, which have been already considered.

But even after all necessary deductions for the Bishop's exaggerations, there can be no question that these facts, taken as a whole, are of a character to incline us to a smaller estimate of the number of the Israelites than that which is inferred from the mention of the 600,000 warriors. The Exodus, indeed, was a miraculous work throughout. The greater miracles in it may therefore seem to imply such lesser ones as might be needed. Yet we are naturally averse to the supposition of miracles not recorded. And so far as the Bishop's reasoning tends merely to clear up a difficult question, and to show what evidence there is in favor of a smaller estimate of the Mosaic census, it is all allowable enough.

I object to it only so far as it is conducted in a narrow, carping, one-sided frame of mind. But, unfortunately, such is the tone of the discussion, from the beginning to the end.

It is in this spirit that the Bishop urges the interesting inquiry as to the *probable increase of Jacob's seventy*, during the time of their sojourn in Egypt. It will be enough to expose two of its fallacies.

First: He scornfully ignores the evidence, which is by no means contemptible, in favor of the longer of the two periods commonly allotted to that sojourn. The shorter period suits his purpose. He *assumes* it, therefore, as the basis of his calculations.

Secondly: He disdainfully rejects, against probabilities of the most natural kind, the idea that *others besides the seventy* may have settled in the land of Goshen. Abraham's "company" was at least 318 men.

Isaac moved as a prince among the princes of Canaan. Jacob was a thrifty man, and lived certainly on good terms with his neighbors the Canaanites. It is highly probable, then, that Jacob, like his great forefathers, had besides his immediate family a large circle of allies or dependents.* The famine which drove him into Egypt would equally touch them; and it would have been the strangest thing in the world if at some time during the seven years of dearth they had not followed him in his migration.

But Bishop Colenso does not find this in the record. Moses does not *say* that any one came to Goshen, either with or after Jacob, save the seventy only. It is a sum in arithmetic based on the number 70, and on the basis of 70 the sum must be cyphered out.

Moreover, these 70 and their descendants must marry in their own family. Bishop Colenso's sum will not suffer them to do otherwise. To be sure, Joseph had married out of the house; as also Simeon, Gen. xlvi. 10: but *it is not written* that any one after them ventured to do the same. Though the daughters in Jacob's List were not sufficient for one thirtieth of the sons, yet *we are not told* that the sons looked for wives elsewhere. It is therefore to be assumed that they did not. The *data* furnished by Moses must be the terms of the calculation. To assume anything beyond is to be guilty of an evasion.

Such is the iron rule, on which Bishop Colenso cyphers out the increase of Jacob's family. Is it to be wondered at that he should bring it to the small amount of less than 5,000 men?

It would be a waste of time to argue against results

---

* See Gen. xxx. 43; xxxiv. 29; xxxv. 5.

based upon such assumptions.* I therefore say nothing of the similar cyphering in Chapters XVIII–XXI. In all such cases, the Bishop's reasoning is merely a repetition of the well-known infidel puzzle,—Gen. iv. 17,— "Whence did Cain get his wife?" If, in a condensed

---

* Though quite unnecessary, I will mention a few more of the *assumptions* made by the Bishop, in cyphering out the increase of Jacob's family. 1. For 215 years he *assumes* only 4 generations, p. 180: whereas, at the rate of 30 years, there would be 7 generations. It is a well-known fact, that a laboring and servile population, like that of the Israelites in Egypt, increase early and rapidly, becoming grandparents not unfrequently before they arrive at 40 years of age. This is particularly the case when the means of subsistence are as plentiful as they would seem to have been in Goshen. 2. He *assumes*, for the rate of increase, the present *English* rate, namely 23 per cent. in 10 years, p. 171: whereas it is well known, that when population begins to press upon the means of subsistence, as is the case in England, the rate of increase very much diminishes. 3. He *assumes* 3 sons for a family, calculating from the families mentioned in Exod. vi., and *assuming* that *all* the children are named, p. 165; or, 4½ sons for a family, calculating from the sons of Jacob, p. 163: whereas, if he had taken a larger basis for his calculations, namely, Abraham, Jokshan, Dedan, Midian, Ishmael, Isaac, Jacob, Esau, Eliphaz, Reuel,—Gen. xxv., xxxvi., &c.,—he would have found an average of $5\tfrac{9}{10}$ sons to a family. 4. He *assumes*, against all probability, that no daughters were born to all these numerous families, except the two or three who are named. 5. He *assumes* that wherever Moses gives names in any connection, as in genealogies and the like, he gives *all* the names. To me nothing is more certain than the contrary. A close study of "the generations" of Moses, beginning with Gen. x., would demonstrate (I think) that the writer was guided by some principle of *selection ;* and that he gives only what I may call *type* names,—that is, names connected in some way with that field of history which he had in view. Abraham, probably, had sons (Gen. xxv. 6) who are casually alluded to but are nowhere named.

and summary history, covering vast intervals, and written for other ends than to gratify curiosity,* we are to suppose nothing to have been done beyond what the writer may have recorded; then, as I have said before, it is not Moses only, but all writers of any merit, that will have to be treated as " unhistorical."

In short, I have given examples enough to show that Bishop Colenso's reasoning depends entirely upon certain things which he assumes; that his assumptions, again, depend upon a stand-point of his own; that, finally, this stand-point is simply that of the infidel; namely, a determination, at all hazards, and in violation of all rules of generous interpretation, to wrest the letter of Scripture to the overthrow of its spirit.

Having given examples of this, I will not follow the subject into its minuter details: but will now go on with the one important question, to wit, How far the difficulties connected with Scripture numbers affect the authority of the sacred writings, as *inspired* and *historical*.

---

* To a Christian mind, the spirit of Moses, as well as "the spirit of prophecy," is "the testimony of Jesus." That Divine instinct which led the historian so to *select* his characters and facts, as to present continually certain *types* or foreshadowings of Christ, is to those who have the eyes to see it an irresistible evidence of the Inspiration of the Scriptures. Without studying this feature of the Mosaic narratives, their harmony and their meaning are in a great measure lost. And I may say in general that he who sees not Christ everywhere in the Old Testament Writings, misses the only proof of their Divine character that can give permanent satisfaction. Not having the true spiritual point-of-view, he fails to discern their spiritual meaning. On the two extremes of interpretation, the *literal* and the *spiritualistic*, see Lee on Inspiration, p. 310, and Appendix G.

XI.

HOW THESE FACTS AFFECT THE BIBLE AS INSPIRED AND HISTORICAL.

IF numerals were used but *vaguely*, in the "old time" of the sacred writers; if they were used in a *mystic* way; if they were peculiarly exposed to *corruption*, whether from accident or from scribes: if, in short, the numerals of the Bible, from one cause or from many, are in such a confused state that we find them inexplicable;*—then, *How does all this affect the Bible as inspired and historical?*

I. I answer, Not at all. Granting the utmost in this way that can possibly be claimed, it merely proves that, out of the great bulk of inspired language in which God's Will is conveyed, there are certain parts which convey to us an imperfect or vague meaning: parts, which in our present state of knowledge we cannot satisfactorily explain.

As these parts relate, moreover, to the modern science of "statistics," and are matters of learned curiosity

* I wish it to be understood, that I put such admissions merely as *hypotheses:* the difficulty, after all, is one that yields easily to a liberal and spiritual system of interpretation.

rather than of the Faith, we may not be quite sure that the key to their interpretation, in a scientific way, will ever be recovered.

But, even so, the admission does not affect the doctrine of Inspiration. In the Bible, as in Nature, there is a superabounding wealth: an ample provision against such losses as may accidentally occur. God inspired men to write with freedom, in the language of their own times. This language, of course, may become in part obscure, and in part unintelligible. The key to some of its idioms may be lost irrecoverably. Yet, as the part which remains clear is still superabundant; as it conveys, and more than conveys, the whole counsel of God: the great end of Inspiration is still most fully answered.

Moreover, these dark places of Scripture may have been light to former ages, whatever they may be to us. They were therefore not words wasted. And even to us they have their uses, both as tokens of extreme antiquity, and as calls to the exercise of the graces of the 131st Psalm.

Were the Bible a clear book, from every point-of-view; were there no idioms in it hard to be understood; were there no proofs of habits of mind, which tax one's powers to the utmost to conceive of and enter into; had it none of the mystic depths of *the child-soul* of that old Semitic world: then, to my mind, at least, it would lack one of its strongest "evidences"; it would be hard for me to receive it as a voice of the "old time" of plenary Inspiration.

Granting the utmost, then, with regard to the difficulties of some places of the Bible, I see in this admission nothing that goes against its claim to be the sure

Word of God. The admission merely proves the folly of "private interpretation." The Bible not being the mind of any individual, but being (2 Pet. i. 20, 21) the broad mind of the Spirit of all Truth, it requires the whole mind of the Church to interpret it with authority. It needs, to make it clear, the learning[*] of all ages. It requires, to make it sure, the stability of that *stand-point* which is provided in the Church.

II. But, if such admissions are made with regard to the Pentateuch, will it not prove, at all events, that the Pentateuch is " unhistorical " ?

In speaking of the Pentateuch as " historical," there are three necessary distinctions to be constantly borne in mind. *First*, it is *ancient* history ; *secondly*, it is *sacred* history ; *thirdly*, it is a history of *supernatural* events.

First : As *ancient* history, it is not to be judged exclusively by modern canons of " the historical ; " for the child-like mind of the old world had habits of its own, and for these peculiar habits a certain allowance must be made.

To illustrate my meaning, I will suppose the case of two witnesses in court. The first is a man of exact and cultivated mind : of a grammatical, mathematical, and logical education. Being such, he gives his evidence lucidly, methodically, with everything in its due order of time and place and logical connection. The second man, equally honest, has no such discipline in his thoughts. He tells his story in bits and parcels, just as it comes into his mind. He is somewhat dramatic in his style. He uses words in a loose or idiomatic way. He some-

---

[*] 2 Pet. iii. 16.

times transposes facts, putting them in the order in which they start out from his memory, rather than in the order in which they actually occur. In short, he gives his evidence inartificially, and the necessary result is somewhat of a medley. Yet, to a lawyer of any shrewdness, this second man's testimony is not the less valuable on that account. Nor is it a whit the less true. On the contrary, if the object is to elicit the whole truth, the second man, it is probable, will actually let out more in his artless and random way, than the utmost skill of the bench and bar can extract from the other witness.

Now modern history is more methodical than the ancient; it is more philosophical, as we say: its testimony runs in grooves more elaborately laid out. Ancient history is, comparatively, inartificial and discursive. It had to run, as it could, without the help of grooves. As a natural consequence, it is oftentimes perplexing. It puts facts out of their place, and puzzles the statistician with all kinds of odd omissions. What is worse, it is often couched in a semi-poetic style, the language of nature not yet broken to the yoke of arithmetic. It abounds in "winged words," which till the wings are clipped disturb the gravity of modern critics, in a way hardly to be endured. In short, like Pindar's poetic "bolts," it "needs an interpreter." Yet, no wise man will contend that ancient history, on the whole, has less truth in it than the modern.[*] It may, of course, be more difficult to ascertain the truth: but to one who reads with his mind, and not merely

---

[*] This subject is admirably discussed by Rawlinson in his Introduction to Herodotus.

with his eyes, the elder chroniclers are, after all, the most veracious of historians.

Secondly: The Bible is *sacred* history, and therein differs materially from that style, with which the word "history" is commonly associated. A secular historian gives events, partly in the order of time and place, partly in that of natural causes and effects. With him man is the chief actor: nature and natural motives, the principal agencies. But the sacred historian begins and ends with God. He exhibits God working in terrestrial affairs. Everything else is strictly subordinate to that. Matters, which from an every-day point-of-view are of principal importance, become from this sacred point-of-view of secondary importance. Hence, while sacred history sometimes deals in facts and figures like other histories, it naturally gives them with less regard to mere statistical effect. It is, therefore, peculiarly liable to omissions of detail. What is not to its purpose it says nothing about. This feature, indeed, is common to all history, and especially to ancient history. But as sacred history involves, more than any other, a certain distinct object and a singular point-of-view, it will naturally for that reason be as remarkable for what it leaves unsaid, as for what it sees fit to mention.

Thirdly: The Bible is a history of *supernatural events.* Its province, therefore, is peculiar and distinct. And as an ordinary historian touches lightly upon miracles, because whether true or not they come hardly within his line, so a sacred historian deals with commonplace events. So far as he mentions them, he does it for the most part lightly and summarily. From his point-of-view they are mere matters of course. Hence, as even ordinary history leaves much to the intelligence of the reader, assuming either a knowledge that will supply details, or at least a liberality that will readily account for their omission, the same, to a far greater extent, may in the case of sacred history be reasonably expected.

With due regard to considerations of this kind, it will be seen that the peculiarities of Moses are not of a character to impair his credit as a historian. At the utmost, they show that like the ancients generally he was indifferent to statistics; that, while he gave certain facts and certain results, he took no special pains to give *all* the facts which were included in his results; that, in the use of numerals especially, he wrote on some system, or in some habit of mind, unintelligible to us; that, in short, there are "some things" in Moses "hard to be understood."

In other words, we are obliged in reading Moses, as in reading Herodotus, to make certain allowances. For example, when in Gen. iv. 17, we read of Cain's *wife*, we conclude that Adam had children not mentioned by the historian: and, having made this natural inference, we draw from it a rule which we are obliged to apply continually to the whole narrative that follows. We conclude, in fact, that Moses leaves many things unsaid, and a still larger number of things totally unaccounted for. But is a feature of this kind "unhistorical"? By no means. A made up story generally shows that it is made up, by accounting for everything. If a new character comes into a novel, the novelist immediately stops his narrative to tell us who this new character is. Fiction, in short, must be complete in itself, because its facts and characters and events have no existence outside of itself. History is never self-complete. From the great living world of facts it reflects certain images, according to some principle of selection, but there is always an infinite number of other images toward which its glass is not directed, and which therefore it does not reflect.

Hence no particular history can be read intelligently, in the full sense of the word, without either a knowledge of *all* history, or at least an imagination which will in some sort supply the defect.

But this faculty of imagination has no place in the cyphering school of such critics as Bishop Colenso. It suggests hypotheses. It hints at the possibility of *data* other than those which are set down on the critic's slate. It spoils the sum. Like a mischievous boy, therefore, it is turned out of school: and Faith, unfortunately, is turned out with it.

To come back, then, to the lowest and most matter-of-fact view: Bishop Colenso finds in Moses some *twenty* supposed difficulties, arising either from apparent contradictions, or from things improbable in themselves. Of these, one or two are *scientific:* but he does not dwell on them; he is content to hint at them occasionally, in order to give weight to his other charges. Two are *moral* difficulties: to wit, a difference of opinion between Moses and the Bishop on the lawfulness of slavery. Some seven or eight are merely *verbal*, founded on perversions of well known idioms, which the Bishop construes on principles that would turn all language into nonsense. The rest are cyphered out by arithmetical calculations, the basis of each sum being the utterly unwarrantable assumption, that the details furnished by a historian must be sufficient to *prove* his general summaries of results. Among all these, there is one which enters as an element also into most of the others, namely, that which is connected with the ancient names or signs of number. But does not this difficulty pertain to all ancient history?* Not to go back at all to the contemporaries of Moses; to say nothing of the round numbers of the Egyptians, or Hindoos or Chinese; but to come down to as late a day as the times of the first Emperors: Who can tell us, *within a million*, the population of Rome? Some put it as low as one million. Others have raised the estimate to nearly seven millions. And if most men now incline to adopt the lower figure, it is rather from the analogy of the census of modern cities, than from any reliable *data* furnished us by the ancients.

The ancients, in fact, knew nothing of statistics, on any large scale. Their histories, therefore, are unreliable on that point. But do we conclude, for such reasons, that ancient histories are "unhistorical?" Or, if we do not, why should we condemn Moses?

I might go on now to speak of that higher ground, and more spiritual point-of-view, from which the early Fathers viewed the subject of Scripture numbers. But it would lead me too far into an abstract and intricate discussion. I pass it by, therefore: and conclude with a few remarks on the great and crowning fallacy of the Skeptics in general.

* The *data* of Herodotus, as well as his sum-total, would make the army of Xerxes more than 5,000,000 men: Grote's Hist. of Greece, Vol. V. See Appendix B.

XII.

CONCLUDING REMARKS: THE CROWNING FALLACY.

The assailant of the Bible has, in one particular, a very easy task. In a question which, like all others, has two sides to it, he feels himself obliged to look to one side only.

This would not be the case with a Skeptic, were he really a Skeptic in the old sense of the word: were he really one who is *looking* or *inquiring* for the Truth. Such a one, of course, knowing that rational conviction must result from the balance of probabilities, would be anxious to weigh well the reasons on both sides: and he would allow no force to arguments against a received opinion, unless he had compared them with the reasons in its favor, and carefully struck a balance between the two.

But Bishop Colenso is not a Skeptic of this kind. He comes out simply as an assailant of the Bible, and feels no responsibility as to what may be said in its defence. His is the easy work of marshalling "difficulties." He loves the cheap triumph of drawing up his forces where there is nothing to oppose them. In the course of his discussion, he manages to bring out some twenty supposed marks of the "unhistorical" character of the Books of Moses: but of the hundreds which have been brought to prove the contrary, he lisps not a syllable. He thus creates an illusion which is vastly in his favor. When only a few points are discussed, it looks as if the controversy turned solely upon them. The reader easily falls into the error, that the battle is between certain " difficulties " on the one side, and on the other certain efforts of commentators to remove or reconcile them: whereas, in fact, the difficult passages in Scripture, even if they were all what the critic tries to prove them, are still immensely overmatched by a host of passages which are not difficult; which testify most plainly and unequivocally to the truth and historical character of the sacred narratives.

The fallacy has been exposed so often, and so ably, that it will be enough, in this Tract, to call attention to it. If any one desires to see the best exposé of it, let him read that wise and witty essay of Archbishop Whately,* entitled " Historic Doubts with regard to the Emperor Napoleon." He will there see how easy it is to disprove anything, by simply ignoring the fact that a question has two sides.

The great controversy in Germany, relative to the existence of a certain character known as Homer, was an example of the same fallacy more seriously carried out. A person of the name of Wolf, if Wolf was a person—for when we speak of these learned Germans, we ought not to be too certain of anything we say:—this person, or "cycle" of persons, that goes by the name of Wolf—a name that seems too *mythic* to be considered

---

* There are others of the Archbishop's works which exhibit the same fallacy, in a more serious way.

5

"historical:"—this person, or myth, or lupine cycle, or whatever he may have been, undertook to prove that the Iliad was not the work of *one poet*—for what poet ever composed an epic equal to that?—but was a kind of joint-stock concern, the result of the accumulated labors of a sort of poetic guild or firm, which flourished for sundry ages under the sunny skies of Greece. The notion was a new one, and the proof of it was easy. Pick out from Homer everything that looks as if it might have been said by somebody else; catch Homer nodding wherever he seems to wink; cull the interpolated verses of which there are not a few; expose the actual contradictions, and add on a few imaginary ones; find words here or there which look too new for Homer's age: in short, bring all the proof you can on one side of the question, and make it appear as if that were the only side: and your work, you may be sure, is satisfactorily accomplished.

Of course, with ancient personages like Homer or Herodotus or Moses, the task is much more easy, than when a Napoleon Bonaparte is taken in hand.

Bishop Colenso's effort is entirely of this cheap and easy character. It is not an inquiry into *the claims* of the Pentateuch. That would imply some examination of the claims. But the Bishop hardly so much as hints that any claims of the kind exist. Nor is it an attempt to disprove *the arguments* which have been framed upon a critical examination of the whole text of the Pentateuch. That would involve some mention of those arguments. The Bishop encumbers himself with nothing of the sort. His aim is not to find the armor-of-proof in which the Bible is encased, but simply to find, if he can, some hole in the armor.

CONCLUSION.

For this reason I have felt no scruple about dealing with the Bishop, as really an Infidel and an enemy of Christianity.

And if I had any scruples on the subject, they would be effectually removed by that shameless avowal of pure heathenism, with which, in his Concluding Remarks, p. 222–226, he sums up his estimate of the Inspiration of the Bible. So far as the Bible utters a certain class of utterances, which "when once perceived by the spirit's eyes, are recognized at once as truths," he grants it to be in some sense inspired. But then, there is a like inspiration all through the world. Consequently, we must "recognize the voice of God's Spirit, in whatever way, by whatever ministry, He vouchsafes to speak to the children of men." Whereupon he gives us, as "living truths . . . . learned by the direct teaching of the Spirit of God," some three pages of Mohammedan and Hindoo aphorisms.

A Christian man may admire what is good in Hindooism, as cordially and as frankly as Bishop Colenso does. He may firmly believe also, that whatever light there is amid the darkness of Heathendom, comes undoubtedly from the Father of Lights. But his conviction is none the less sure that the only "true Light," "the Light of men," is He, the everlasting Word, who was manifested, and "was made flesh, and dwelt among us . . . . full of grace and truth." Without belief in a historic Christ, no man can be called in any sense a Christian. And no man can believe in Christ, as an historic Personage, without faith in Moses and the Prophets who were inspired by the Holy Ghost to bear testimony of Him.

This Divine Word Incarnate, this manifested Truth,

this Emmanuel, God with us, Bishop Colenso has abandoned, or what amounts to the same thing, is ready to abandon. And all for what? He solemnly assures us that it is all for the sake of "truth." But what truth has he found? What precious discovery does he offer us, to supply the place of that inheritance which he would fain take away? A few fatalistic maxims, Mohammedan or Hindoo, the feeble common-places of natural theology, words true in a certain sense, but without power, without grace, without life, the mere roundings as it were of Ciceronian periods, the thin veil of a religion without faith, without hope, without God in the world. Is this a fair equivalent for that Gospel, which is not in word only, but in power?

I can only say, God have mercy on the soul which can imagine it an equivalent: which can see no difference between the Day-Star of Christianity, and the vague and feeble lights which reveal, but do not illumine, the darkness of Heathendom!

APPENDIX A.

NUMBER OF THE FIRST-BORN, &c.

(*See p.* 71.)

THE best way (perhaps) of reconciling the number of the "first-born" with that of the male adults is suggested by the fact, that the total number of Levites was 22,300—as the reader will see by adding up the partial estimates in Num. iii. 22, 28, 34—whereas only 22,000 were available as *substitutes* for the first-born. What became, then, of the 300 ? It is answered, that they were the *first-born of the Levites*, and consequently could only redeem themselves, and not their brethren. If so, the first-born of the Levites (born since the Passover) would be in the proportion of 300 to 22,000, or of 1 to 74 of the males "from a month old and upward": Num. iii. 15. Now, supposing that the first-born of the other tribes meant only those who had been born *since the Law of Redemption had been instituted*, we may make the following calculation: 600,000 fighting men would be about $\frac{1}{2}$ or $\frac{1}{3}$ of the male population of all ages: if we allow $\frac{1}{2}$, the total number would be 1,200,000; if we allow $\frac{1}{3}$, it would be 1,800,000. Divide these sums respectively by 22,000, the number of first-born, and we get the rate of 1 to 55 in the one case, and 1 to 81 in the other: or, if we take the warriors to be (as is probable) something more than $\frac{1}{3}$ and less than $\frac{1}{2}$ of the whole number of males, we get a close approximation to the 1 in 74 which has been previously calculated as the proportion of first-born among the Levites.

From this coincidence arises a probability, that the first-born in Num. iii. 43, were only those who had been born *since* the Law of Redemption had been given; and that said Law was not intended to have a retrospective force.

These hypotheses—which are certainly not more violent than the assumptions of Bishop Colenso—would put the 22,000 first-born and the 600,000 warriors in a fairer proportion to one another; and so far would relieve the chief difficulty: see Poole's *Synopsis*, in Num. iii. 39.

Even if we take the higher of the two rates above mentioned, and suppose the warriors to be $\frac{1}{4}$ the male population, the proportion of the first-born, namely 1 to 55, would be greater than the 1 to 74 of the Levites; but the difference might be accounted for by the probable supposition, that the Levites being more restricted *in marriage* than the other tribes, there would consequently have been fewer births among them.

The chief difficulty in the way of such hypotheses is that the 22,273 in Num. iii. 43, are described as "*all* the first-born males, &c." But the whole analogy of Scripture language shows, that the word "all" has no absolute force, but is to be taken always in reference to the general scope of the context in which it is used. "All the first-born males," in this instance, means *all who came under the Law of Redemption:* and it is probable enough, that none came under it but those who had been "born" under it—namely, those who had been born since the Passover.

Considerations of this kind would enable us to get rid of the seeming *discrepancy* in the numbers used by Moses.

The other instances of discrepancy, cited by Bishop Colenso, are easily enough accounted for, on general principles. For example, the census referred to in Exod. xxxviii. 26, exactly *tallies* with the census taken 6 months after in Num. i. The Bishop asks, How could this be? Was there no increase of population the meanwhile? I answer, The returns of the second census being made by the "heads of thousands" (i. 16), with a view to the *military* enrolment (chap. ii.), there would be no need of a fresh count: the numbering that had taken place 6 months before would be sufficient to satisfy the veriest Martinet. But why take a fresh census at all? Why could not Moses be content with the returns of the former numbering? I answer, The former returns were made in *connection with the tribute* of bekahs, and were therefore made probably by tribes. Moses wished a new return made (Num. i. 3) "by armies": *i. e.* by such military divisions, *thousands, hundreds, fifties, tens*, as were in vogue among them. This would require not a new numbering of the people, but merely a new arrangement of the census previously taken.

The diminished number of the last census taken, Num. xxvi. 51, is amply accounted for by the great number who had fallen in the wilderness.

On the whole, the difficulty arising from the seeming discrepancies of the numbers in the Pentateuch disappear before a fair and liberal interpretation.

But in proportion as the discrepancies are removed, the claims of the higher numbers seem to be strengthened; and the considerations which I have urged in the text, with a view to a possible reduction of them, appear in the same ratio to lose their force.

As to that, I am not at all solicitous: for the Israelites, whatever their number may have been, were sustained in the wilderness by miraculous power; and a great miracle is to my mind as easy as a small one. If God could send *manna* and *quails* for 10,000 people, He could just as easily provide the same food for 10,000,000. And if He could provide for the people, He could as easily provide for the cattle. A supernatural act implies an absolute power to perform all that is necessary for the completeness of that act. If the sun stood still at Joshua's command, the same Power which arrested the earth's motion—or did anything else that might be needed to keep the sun from going down—would prevent any damage that might ensue from such an arrest. So far as natural laws go, they are as powerful to keep a dead body in the grave, as to keep the planets in their spheres. And on the same principle, so far as the Divine Power manifests itself, it is as mighty to reverse the main-wheel of the world as it is to call forth a Lazarus from the tomb.

I do not incline to the lower numbers, therefore, for any supposed difficulty about sustaining so great a multitude of people. The whole Pentateuch puts this on the ground of miracle. My main reason for admitting the possibility of a smaller estimate is, that the whole subject of ancient numbers, and of Scripture interpretation as connected with them, is extremely intricate and perplexed. It is one that involves much more than the text of Moses. Moreover, it is one which interpreters (so far as I can find) have not studied as thoroughly and systematically as its importance demands. In fact, Bible arithmetic is somewhat of a new science. It is well, therefore, not to commit one's self to *any* theory on the subject, until all that bears upon it has been subjected to that kind of analysis in which the modern mind excels; and which is never honestly applied, either to Scripture or to Nature, without yielding good fruit in the end.

Lee, in the Eighth Lecture of his learned work on Inspiration, gives some striking instances to show that such analysis of the difficulties of Scripture never fails, in the long run, to bring out something whereby the consistency of the Divine Word is more fully proved.

In short, I do not offer any solution of the difficulties connected with numbers: I merely wish to show that the question is too difficult to be dealt with in any such summary fashion as that of Bishop Colenso. If interpretation is a *science*, requiring both tact and learning, there is no branch of it that requires so much of both as that of Scriptural numeration.

APPENDIX B.

NUMBERS IN HERODOTUS.

(*See p.* 95.)

It may be doubted whether the historian ever took more pains to ascertain and record the truth, than when he compiled the list of Xerxes's army. He not only gives the number of each contingent, with particular accounts of the nation from which it came, but for once in his life adds up the whole correctly, to the enormous sum total of 5,283,320. As a general rule, the arithmetic of Herodotus is very loose. "If both the items and the total of a sum are mentioned, they are rather more likely to disagree than to agree; . . . . either he was not an adept in arithmetic, or he did not take the trouble to go through the calculations, and see that his statements tallied": Rawlinson's Herod., vol. i. p. 84. But the account of the host of Xerxes exhibits the utmost care in this respect.

Rawlinson, upon a careful examination of the items, and after a heavy reduction of those numbers which Herodotus had *estimated* or *conjectured*, manages to bring the total down to 1,531,610 : vol. iii. p. 129.

Considering the immense difficulty of bringing together, moving and feeding, large bodies of men, even with the strict discipline and great facilities of modern times, Rawlinson's reduced estimate seems a little less impossible, but hardly more probable, than that of Herodotus. Napoleon, the greatest military genius of modern times, fairly broke down in the attempt to move an army of 500,000. Xerxes was no genius; and his forces were a conglomeration of the mobs of all nations, a Babel of diverse tongues, utterly unaccustomed to act together on any large scale. How such a host, wielded by such a man, could have been kept together for a month, is extremely difficult to imagine. What is worse, I can see no practical diminution of the difficulty, unless one should boldly cut down the estimate to less than one-third of Rawlinson's, or one-tenth of that which Herodotus gives. An army of half a million would be such as a commander like Xerxes might keep for some time in a state of *retarded* dissolution, but for any other purpose it would be quite unmanageable.

Yet, of the honesty and good faith of Herodotus I have no doubt whatever. The enormous exaggeration was due, in all probability, to the loose way of counting that prevailed everywhere, and especially in the East. When men got beyond hundreds, imagination took the slate, and the cyphering went on by leaps into thousands and myriads, with little or no check from sober reason. The round numbers, in short, were used so much as figures of speech, that their mathematical import was almost forgotten.

APPENDIX C.

PARALLELISM IN NUMBERS.

In Browne's "Introduction" to his *Ordo Sæclorum*, the "parallelisms" of Bible Chronology are pointed out; and it is shown that while a *design* is apparent, the design is such as cannot be accounted for by any theory of *human* contrivance. Thus, we have: 40 years in the wilderness followed by 450 years of Judges, in all 490 years; 40 years from Samuel the first of the *Prophets*, with 450 years of kings, in all 490 years; the 70 years of captivity, in which "the land kept her Sabbaths;" then the seventy times seven years of Daniel, 490 years. Again, the length of the Mosaic Period is 1655 years; the sum of the antediluvian genealogies is 1655 years; from the time that Noah entered the Ark to the promise given to Abraham is 430 years; from the promise to the Exodus is 430 years: or, from the Creation to the Promise is 2085 years;

from the Promise to the end of the Mosaic Dispensation is 2085 years. Upon these and similar coincidences Browne remarks : " The notion of human contrivance being excluded, is it presumptuous to surmise that this is the Lord's doing, a portion of His ways, who doeth all in number, weight and measure," &c. ? His reasoning on this subject is well worth considering, and is capable of a broader application than that which he gives. On the mystic use of numbers, the following from Joh. Picus Mirandula, quoted in the *Bibliotheca Biblica*, vol. iv. p. 9, may be interesting to the reader. " Besides our *new* method of philosophizing by numbers "—I translate freely —" there is an ancient way, followed by the early Divines, and more especially by Pythagoras, . . . by Plato and the elder Platonists. At present, however, like other good things, it has so fallen into disuse through the negligence of moderns, that hardly any traces of it can be found. Says Plato in the Epimenides, Among all the liberal arts and theoretic sciences, the principal and most Divine is the science of numbers. So again, when asked, Why is man the wisest of living things? he answers, Because he is acquainted with numbers. . . . So also Abunasar declares, that he knows everything who knows the science of numbers. But by this is not to be understood that kind of arithmetic in which men of business are skilled : for Plato expressly warns us, that this Divine Arithmetic is not at all the same as the arithmetic of commerce," &c. &c.

APPENDIX D.

GENEALOGIES OF THE SCRIPTURES.

The Genealogies of Scripture are particularly open to the captious criticism of such writers as Bishop Colenso: partly because they are constructed, as is obvious to the most cursory reader, on some principle of *selection*, and partly because names, like numbers, are peculiarly liable to corruption. Thus, if we suppose Moses, in Exod. vi. 16–25, to have given a complete list of the family of Levi, the large numbers assigned to that tribe in Num. iii. 17–39 seem as incredible as the Bishop represents them: Chap. XVIII. But the list is evidently *not* complete. "These be the *heads* of their fathers' houses. . . . . . according to their families. . . . These are the families according to their generations. . . . These *the heads of the fathers* of the Levites, according to their families": Exod. vi. 14–25. All which expressions plainly imply that Moses gives only certain prominent representative names: a thing so common in Scripture genealogies, that we may doubt whether in any case an entire family list is recorded. The very small proportion of *women*, in all these lists, would suggest at once that a large number of names is omitted. Thus, among all the descendants of Esau, Gen. xxxvi., I find but one daughter, ver. 26. So, in Gen. xlvi., there are but two daughters. In the former case there is every reason to suppose that the *one* daughter mentioned was recorded for some special reason, and that there were plenty of others not thus honored. In the latter instance, the two daughters *may* have been all that were born to Jacob and his sons; and the phrase, "all the souls of his sons and daughters (were)" so and so, looks as if it were meant to include all. Yet it does not say they "*were*" all: the verb is not in the original; and the sentence in which it occurs is manifestly a mere summing up of names actually given, and has no force beyond: Gen. xlvi. 15, 18, 26, 27. So, among the hundreds of sons named in 1 Chron. vi.–ix., there are not more than ten daughters mentioned.

Again, among all the names and genealogies in the first *eleven* chapters of Genesis, there are but five names of women. It is perfectly evident, therefore, that with regard to one sex at least the genealogies deal only in representative names.

The variations that exist among the genealogies show that the same applies also to the other sex: names being found in one genealogy which are not given in others. Thus St. Matthew's genealogy of our Lord omits several names, which the Old Testament enables us to supply: see Newcome's Harmony.

We have a perfect right, therefore, to conclude that, when Moses mentions certain persons as "heads of the fathers of the Levites," or uses other like expressions, he is giving us only the prominent, historical, representative names. To give more in any history, sacred or profane, would be a useless labor. It is still more idle to attempt, as Bishop Colenso does, to calculate from the names given the populousness of the tribes or families that they represent. The fathers, "heads of fathers," or *chief* fathers of nations, who find a place in history are very few indeed, compared with the number of actual progenitors.

APPENDIX E.
THE GENEALOGY OF JOSHUA.

THE genealogy of Joshua, 1 Chron. vii. 20–27, might seem at first sight to involve the stupidities and absurdities which Bishop Colenso attempts to draw out from it; p. 158: namely, "that Ephraim himself, after the slaughter by the men of Gath of his descendants in the *seventh* generation, 'mourned many days,' and then married again, and had a son, Beriah, who was the ancestor of Joshua;" or that "Joshua will be made a descendant in the *seventeenth* generation from Joseph, to associate with Eleazar in the *fourth* generation from Levi."

A critic of any modesty at all, would pause a moment before charging an ancient writer with such stupidity, lest perchance the absurdity should come home to roost in his own interpretation, and put the fool's cap upon his own head.

And a moment's pause would be sufficient to show that Bishop Colenso's interpretation has not even the poor excuse of adhering to the bare letter. He has not only failed to read with his mind, but even his eyes, in this instance, have failed to serve him. Ephraim's family list, as is common enough in Scripture, contains several genealogies alongside of one another. It begins with *Shuthelah*, the first-born, and then goes on with "*his* son," and "*his* son," and so on for six generations: it then comes back to the second and third sons of Ephraim, "*Ezer* and *Elead*, whom the men of Gath slew because they came down to take their cattle:" it then relates the birth of a fourth son of Ephraim, *Beriah*, and proceeds with "*his* son," and so on: finally, as Browne ingeniously shows in his *Ordo Sæclorum*, it gives (by a sudden and somewhat obscure transition) a fifth son of Ephraim, *Edan* or *Eran*, and comes to Joshua in the fourth generation from him: so that, really, Joshua stands in the fifth generation from Ephraim. This the reader will readily perceive, if he will observe that the *sons* of Ephraim are connected by the copulative "and," or something equivalent, while the grandsons and other lineal descendants are distinguished by the phrase "and *his* son." I will give the whole passage, so arranging it as to make the transitions from sons to descendants, or the reverse, more obvious to the eye.

"And the sons of Ephraim:

"*Shuthelah* ;—

    and Bered *his* son,
    and Tahath *his* son,
    and Eladah *his* son,
    and Tahath *his* son,
    and Zabad *his* son,
    and Shuthelah *his* son :—

"and *Ezer* and *Elead*, whom the men of Gath that were born in that land slew, because they came down to take away their cattle. And Ephraim their father mourned many days, and his brethren came to comfort him. And when he went in to his wife, she conceived and bare a son, and he called his name *Beriah:* because it went evil with his house. (And his daughter was Sheran, who built Beth-horon the nether, and the upper, and Uzzen-sherah.)

"And Rephah was *his* son, also Resheph,
and Telah *his* son
and Tahan *his* son:"—

Here, according to the LXX, there is another transition to Ephraim's immediate family, marked by *the dative case*, and by putting the word "son" in a different *order:* thus, *verbatim*,
"To *Laadan* his son,
a son Ammihud,
a son Elishama,
a son Non,
a son Jehoshua, his sons."

Browne conjectures that the "L" in the name Laadan is merely the Hebrew preposition, corresponding to the dative case which is given in the Greek: so that the name should read "*to* Adan" or "Edan." And as the "D" and "R" in Hebrew are often mistaken for one another (being much alike) this *Edan* is the same as *Eran*, or *Eden* according to the LXX, one of Ephraim's sons in Num. xxvi. 36. Every one knows that names, in so ancient a language as the Hebrew, are peculiarly exposed to changes at the hands of transcribers or translators; and in this instance the Septuagint seems to *indicate*, though not to clear up altogether, some mistake with regard to the name that is rendered Laadan.

Browne's conjecture, therefore, is a highly reasonable one, well supported by analogous cases; and we may complete the genealogy thus:

"To Edan or Eran (Ephraim's) son was
Ammihud *his* son,
Elishama *his* son,
Non *his* son,
Jehoshua *his* son."

(To an English reader I may illustrate the supposed change in the name Laadan somewhat in this way. Suppose the word to have been written originally L D N. A translator into Greek, knowing that the L is often a mere prefix meaning *To*, and guided perhaps by a traditional interpretation, would render the name *To* aDaN; and (to make all sure) would put the original LaaDaN in the margin. Afterward the marginal reading would creep into the text without displacing the sign of the dative; and thus it would come to be, as it stands now in the LXX, To LaaDaN. For examples of the confusion often made between the Hebrew D and R, see 1 Chron. i. 6, 7; where Riphath reads in the margin Diphath, and Dodanim becomes Rodanim. So, in ver. 30, Hadad in the margin reads Hadar. For other changes of the kind, Homam into Heman, Amram into Hemdan, Zimri into Zabdi, Chelubai into Caleb, Eliada into Beeliada, &c., &c., see marginal readings of 1 Chron. i.-x.)

But however this may be, the special absurdities so triumphantly paraded by Bishop Colenso, only serve to prove his own fatuity. Take the list merely as it stands in the English version, and it is obvious at a glance, that *Shuthelah*, *Ezer*, *Elead*, *Beriah* are sons of Ephraim, separated only by the incidental mention of the lineal descendants of Shuthelah, not by any intervention of *seven* generations or *seventeen* generations, such as the Bishop supposes. It is also worth noticing that the fact of the two sons being slain by some men of Gath "*born in the land*" suggests at once an idea very probable in itself, but disdainfully rejected by Bishop Colenso, namely, that some of Jacob's former neighbors, following his example, had migrated from Canaan to Goshen: so that the seventy who went with him into Egypt were gradually reënforced by a numerous immigration. The incidental mention of that "daughter, Sheran, who built Beth-horon," &c., would indicate, that occasionally, among the descendants of Jacob, there was a return to Canaan: perhaps in consequence of intermarriage with settlers or visitors from that region. So far from proving therefore any such absurdities as Bishop Colenso charges upon it, the genealogy in Chronicles really throws much light upon facts which Moses, in his brief narrative, does not see fit to explain.

The only difficulty that remains, namely, (as it appears in our version,) the *nine* generations between Ephraim and Joshua, disappears entirely, if Browne's conjecture be admitted. For in that case, Joshua stands as the *fifth* from Ephraim: while in the two other families, Shuthelah II. is the *seventh* and Tahan the *fourth;* all which is probable and consistent.

This interpretation also enables us to reconcile the genealogy in 1 Chron. with that which is given in Num. xxvi. 35, 36: but for this I refer the reader to Browne, p. 307 : * a writer, by the way, who, if he had had the good fortune to have a *diæresis* over his name, or a *berg* at the end of it, would be in much higher honor among us, and would be more diligently read than at present is the case. We, who speak the English tongue, have a wonderful veneration for the long names and showy learning of the Germans. The plain home-spun of sound English good sense we care little for.

I may add, in passing, that German commentators, whom

---

* I will give the passage *verbatim* from the LXX: in which the reader will note that the cRaN of our version reads cDeN.

"And these sons of Ephraim. To Suthala, the people Suthalai. To Tanach, the people Tanachi: *these sons of Suthala.* To Eden, the people Edeni. These sons of Ephraim by their census."

Here Eden is mentioned, like the Edan or Laadan of Chronicles, in an abrupt way, as if he were too well known to require particular description: which would be natural enough if he was a son of Ephraim and the ancestor of Joshua, but would otherwise be unaccountable. The reader will also note the exact correspondence of the words To eDeN with the Hebrew LDN mentioned above.

Bishop Colenso delights to quote so far as they serve his purpose of making the Scriptures ridiculous, may be very learned men, and prodigiously profound, but are by no means the best authorities to go to, if we wish to have *light* shed upon a difficulty in Scripture. They are critics of that kind who, if they do not love darkness rather than light, yet undoubtedly show a fondness for certain shades of obscurity. They are so absorbed in remote speculations, that they seldom see what is immediately before their eyes. This is the case with Kuenen, whom Bishop Colenso cites, p. 158, in connection with the genealogy of Joshua. The theory that he broaches is only a shade less stupid than that of the Bishop himself. Not having his work before me, however, I am not by any means sure that his meaning is correctly given. At least, in the case of others whom the Bishop quotes and answers, he sometimes selects the point of attack: choosing their feeble and improbable explanations, and omitting those which shed some light on the subject. Whether this has been done in the case of Kuenen I have not as yet ascertained.

D. APPLETON & CO.'S PUBLICATIONS.

Aids to Faith:
A SERIES OF THEOLOGICAL ESSAYS.

By VARIOUS WRITERS.

Being a Reply to "ESSAYS AND REVIEWS."

1 vol., 12mo, cloth, 538 pages, $1.25.

CONTENTS.

I. *On Miracles as Evidences of Christianity.* — H. L. MANSEL, B. D., Waynflete Professor of Moral and Metaphysical Philosophy, Oxford; late Tutor and Fellow of St. John's Coll.

II. *On the Study of the Evidences of Christianity.* — WILLIAM FITZGERALD, D. D., Lord Bishop of Killaloe.

III. *Prophecy* .... — A. M'CAUL, D.D., Professor of Hebrew and Old Testament Exegesis, King's College, London, and Prebendary of St. Paul's.

IV. *Ideology and Subscription* .... — F. C. COOKE, M.A., Chaplain in Ordinary to the Queen, one of H. M. Inspectors of Schools, Prebendary of St. Paul's, and Examining Chaplain to the Bishop of Lincoln.

V. *The Mosaic Record of Creation* ... — A. M'CAUL, D.D., Professor of Hebrew and Old Testament Exegesis, King's College, London, and Prebendary of St. Paul's.

VI. *On the Genuineness and Authenticity of the Pentateuch.* — GEORGE RAWLINSON, M.A., Camden Professor of Ancient History, Oxford; and late Fellow and Tutor of Exeter Coll.

VII. *Inspiration* .... — EDWARD HAROLD BROWNE, B. D., Norrisian Professor of Divinity at Cambridge, and Canon Residentiary of Exeter Cathedral.

VIII. *The Death of Christ.* .... — WILLIAM THOMSON, D. D., Lord Bishop of Gloucester and Bristol.

IX. *Scripture and its Interpretation* ... — CHARLES JOHN ELLICOTT, B. D., Dean of Exeter, and Professor of Divinity, King's College, London.

EXTRACT FROM PREFACE.

This volume is humbly offered to the great Head of the Church, as one attempt among many to keep men true to Him in a time of much doubt and trial. Under His protection, His people need not be afraid. The old difficulties and objections are revived, but they will meet in one way or another the old defeat. While the world lasts skeptical books will be written and answered, and the books, perhaps, and the answers alike forgotten. But the Rock of Ages shall stand unchangeable; and men, worn with a sense of sin, shall still find rest under the shadow of a great rock in a weary land.

HISTORY
OF
CIVILIZATION IN ENGLAND.

By HENRY THOMAS BUCKLE.

2 Vols. 8vo, Cloth. $5.

(From the Boston Journal.)

"Singularly acute, possessed of rare analytical power, imaginative but not fanciful, unwearied in research, and gifted with wonderful talent in arranging and moulding his material, the author is as fascinating as he is learned. His erudition is immense—so immense as not to be cumbersome. It is the result of a long and steady growth—a part of himself.

(From the Chicago Home Journal.)

"The master-stroke of the first volume is the author's skill and success in delineating the train of causes which resulted in the early French Revolution (1793). These causes, with their combinations, are so arranged that the mind of the reader is prepared for results not very unlike such as actually occurred, horrible as they were.

(From the Boston Transcript.)

"His first volume evinces a clear head, an intrepid heart, and an honest purpose. A true kind of induction characterizes it. Indeed it is almost a new revelation, comprising the fidelity of Gibbon, the comprehensiveness of Humboldt, and the fascination of Macaulay."

(From the N. Y. Daily Times.)

"We have read Mr. Buckle's volumes with the deepest interest. We owe him a profound debt of gratitude. His influence on the thought of the present age cannot but be enormous, and if he gives us no more than we already have in the two volumes of the *magnus opus*, he will still be classed among the fathers and founders of the Science of History."

(From the Newark Daily Advertiser.)

"The book is a treat, and even 'mid the din of battle it will be extensively read, for it bears no little upon our own selves, our country, and its future existence and progress."

D. APPLETON & CO.'S PUBLICATIONS.

NEARLY COMPLETE.

THE

New American Cyclopædia,

A POPULAR DICTIONARY OF GENERAL KNOWLEDGE,

EDITED BY

GEORGE RIPLEY AND C. A. DANA,

ASSISTED BY A NUMEROUS BUT SELECT CORPS OF WRITERS.

The design of the NEW AMERICAN CYCLOPÆDIA is to furnish the great body of intelligent readers in this country with a popular Dictionary of General Knowledge.

THE NEW AMERICAN CYCLOPÆDIA is not founded on any European model; in its plan and elaboration it is strictly original, and strictly American. Many of the writers employed on the work have enriched it with their personal researches, observations, and discoveries; and every article has been written, or re-written, expressly for its pages.

It is intended that the work shall bear such a character of practical utility as to make it indispensable to every American library.

Throughout its successive volumes, THE NEW AMERICAN CYCLOPÆDIA will present a fund of accurate and copious information on SCIENCE, ART, AGRICULTURE, COMMERCE, MANUFACTURES, LAW, MEDICINE, LITERATURE, PHILOSOPHY, MATHEMATICS, ASTRONOMY, HISTORY, BIOGRAPHY, GEOGRAPHY, RELIGION, POLITICS, TRAVELS, CHEMISTRY, MECHANICS, INVENTIONS, and TRADES.

Abstaining from all doctrinal discussions, from all sectional and sectarian arguments, it will maintain the position of absolute impartiality on the great controverted questions which have divided opinions in every age.

PRICE.

This work is published exclusively by subscription, in sixteen large octavo volumes, each containing 750 two-column pages. Vols. I. to XIV. are now ready. Price per volume, cloth, $3; library style, leather, $3 50; half morocco, $4; half russia, extra, $4 50.

D. APPLETON & CO.'S PUBLICATIONS.

AN IMPORTANT REFERENCE BOOK.

THE

American Annual Cyclopædia

AND

REGISTER OF IMPORTANT EVENTS OF THE YEAR

1861.

EMBRACING POLITICAL, CIVIL, MILITARY, AND SOCIAL AFFAIRS; PUBLIC DOCUMENTS; BIOGRAPHY, STATISTICS, COMMERCE, FINANCE, LITERATURE, SCIENCE, AGRICULTURE, AND MECHANICAL INDUSTRY.

In our view an Annual Cyclopædia or Register should embrace, as its name implies, the entire circle of important knowledge transpiring during the year; —not merely those movements of power and strength which are the current events in the administration of political and civil affairs; or the deeds of military prowess, whether illustrating the strategy of commanders, or the bravery of soldiers; but the discoveries in science detected by the still thoughts of investigating minds; the portraits of character acted out under the inspiration of virtuous and noble purposes; those countless actions of busy men expressed in the figures of commerce and statistics; the skilful and precise steps of finance, imparting vigor to enterprise and government; the improvements in agriculture and the developments of mechanical genius and industry.

The form of a Cyclopædia has been selected, as affording room for the greatest variety of details, without becoming too minute and tedious. The work is already in an advanced stage of preparation, and will be issued as early in the year as its proper completion will permit. The volume will be in the style of the New American Cyclopædia, having not less than 750 pages, royal 8vo.

The work will be published exclusively by subscription, and in exterior appearance will be at once elegant and substantial.

PRICES AND STYLES OF BINDING.

In Cloth, $3; in Library Style, leather, $3 50; in Half Morocco, plain, $4; in Half Russia, extra, $4 50. Payable on delivery.

D. Appleton & Company's Publications.

18 CHRISTIAN CENTURIES.

BY

THE REV. JAMES WHITE,

AUTHOR OF A HISTORY OF FRANCE.

1 Vol. 12mo. Cloth. 538 pages. $1 25.

CONTENTS.

1. Cent.—The Bad Emperors.—II. The Good Emperors.—III. Anarchy and Confusion.—Growth of the Christian Church.—IV. The Removal to Constantinople.—Establishment of Christianity.—Apostasy of Julian.—Settlement of the Goths.—V. End of the Roman Empire.—Formation of Modern States.—Growth of Ecclesiastical Authority.—VI. Belisarius and Narses in Italy—Settlement of the Lombards.—Laws of Justinian.—Birth of Mohammed.—VII. Power of Rome supported by the Monks.—Conquests of the Mohammedans.—VIII. Temporal Power of the Popes.—The Empire of Charlemagne.—IX.—Dismemberment of Charlemagne's Empire.—Danish Invasion of England.—Weakness of France.—Reign of Alfred.—X. Darkness and Despair.—XI. The Commencement of Improvement.—Gregory the Seventh.—First Crusade.—XII. Elevation of Learning.—Power of the Church.—Thomas à Becket.—XIII. First Crusade against Heretics.—The Albigenses.—Magna Charta.—Edward I.—XIV. Abolition of the Order of Templars.—Rise of Modern Literature.—Schism of the Church.—XV. Decline of Feudalism.—Agincourt.—Joan of Arc.—The Printing Press.—Discovery of America.—XVI. The Reformation.—The Jesuits.—Policy of Elizabeth.—XVII. English Rebellion and Revolution.—Despotism of Louis the Fourteenth.—XVIII. India.—America.—France.—Index.

OPINIONS OF THE PRESS.

Mr. White possesses in a high degree the power of epitomizing—that faculty which enables him to distil the essence from a mass of facts, and to condense it in description; a battle, siege, or other remarkable event, which, without his skill, might occupy a chapter, is compressed within the compass of a page or two, and this without the sacrifice of any feature essential or significant.—CENTURY.

Mr. White has been very happy in touching upon the salient points in the history of each century in the Christian era, and yet has avoided making his work a mere bald analysis or chronological table.—PROV. JOURNAL.

In no single volume of English literature can so satisfying and clear an idea of the historical character of these eighteen centuries be obtained.—HOME JOURNAL.

In this volume we have THE BEST EPITOME OF CHRISTIAN HISTORY EXTANT. This is high praise, but at the same time JUST. The author's peculiar success is in making the great points and facts of history stand out in sharp relief. His style may be said to be STEREOSCOPIC, and the effect is exceedingly impressive.—PROVIDENCE PRESS.

D. Appleton & Company's Publications.

MODERN BRITISH ESSAYISTS,

COMPRISING

The Critical & Miscellaneous Works

OF

ALISON, **CARLYLE,**
JEFFREY, **MACAULAY,**
MACKINTOSH, **SYDNEY SMITH,**
STEPHEN, **TALFOURD,**

And Prof. **WILSON.**

In 8 vols., large 8vo., uniform Cloth, $13. Sheep, $17 Half Calf Ext., $25.

Each Volume to be had separately.

Alison's Essays.
Miscellaneous Essays. By ARCHIBALD ALISON, F. R. S. Reprinted from the English originals, with the author's corrections for this edition. 1 large vol. 8vo. Portrait. Cloth, $1 25; sheep, $1 75.

Carlyle's Essays.
Critical and Miscellaneous Essays. By THOMAS CARLYLE. Complete in one volume. 1 large vol. 8vo. Portrait. Cloth, $2; sheep, $2 50.

Jeffrey's Essays.
Contributions to the Edinburgh Review. By FRANCIS JEFFREY. The four volumes complete in one. 1 very large vol. 8vo. Portrait. Cloth, $2; sheep, $2 50.

Macaulay's Essays.
Essays, Critical and Miscellaneous. By T. BABINGTON MACAULAY. New and Revised edition. 1 very large vol. 8vo. Portrait. Cloth, $2; sheep, $2 50.

Mackintosh's Essays.
The Miscellaneous Works of the Right Honorable Sir JAMES MACKINTOSH. The three volumes in one. 1 vol. large 8vo. Portrait. Cloth, $2; sheep, $2 50.

Sydney Smith's Works.
The Works of the Rev. SYDNEY SMITH. Three volumes complete in one. 1 large vol. 8vo. Portrait. Cloth, $1 25; sheep, $1 75.

Talfourd's and Stephen's Essays.
Critical and Miscellaneous Writings of T. NOON TALFOURD, author of "Ion," &c. Critical and Miscellaneous Essays of JAMES STEPHEN. In 1 vol. large 8vo. Portrait. Cloth, $1 25; sheep, $1 75.

Wilson's Essays.
The Recreations of CHRISTOPHER NORTH [Prof. JOHN WILSON.] Complete in 1 vol. large 8vo. Portrait. Cloth, $1 25; sheep, $1 75.

www.ingramcontent.com/pod-product-compliance
Lightning Source LLC
Chambersburg PA
CBHW020129170426
43199CB00010B/702